14.99

D0996611

Catalonia

Catalonia

Portrait of a Nation

John Payne

CENTURY
London   Sydney   Auckland   Johannesburg

First published in 1991 by Century
Random Century Ltd
20 Vauxhall Bridge Road, London SW1V 2SA

Random Century Australia (Pty) Ltd
20 Alfred Street, Milsons Point, Sydney, NSW 2061, Australia

Random Century New Zealand Ltd
18 Poland Road, Glenfield, Auckland 10, New Zealand

Random Century South Africa (Pty) Ltd
PO Box 337, Bergvlei 2012, South Africa

Set in Linotronic Palatino by CentraCet, Cambridge
Printed and bound in U.K. by Mackays of Chatham Ltd, Chatham, Kent

A catalogue record for this book is available from the British Library

ISBN 0-7126-3826-1

Maps drawn by Mary E. Mackenzie

Contents

Maps

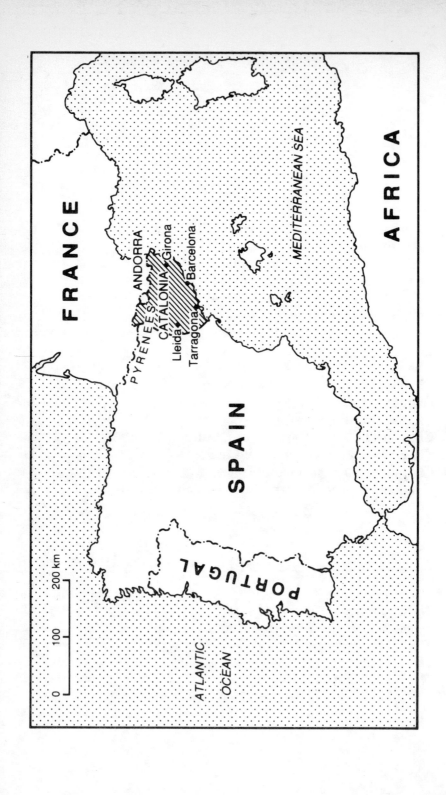

To Lolita and Xavier Muñoz

Acknowledgements

My thanks are due to the many people who contributed their words, ideas and opinions to this book. Some of them are mentioned by name in the text, but also I want to thank the staff of the various tourist offices in Catalonia for their invaluable help, and the staff of the libraries of the Hispanic Council and Spanish Institute in London. Various people, including my own family, have kept me company at different stages of my travels through Catalonia, and their good company, love and friendship have formed an essential backdrop to the scenes and places I describe. Mary Mackenzie's beautifully drawn maps will help the reader to locate the places referred to in the text. At Century, I would like to thank Mark Booth for his support and meticulous editing, and Kayte Nunn who has supervised the production of *Catalonia*.

Preface

Camilo José Cela, the Spanish winner of the Nobel Prize for literature in 1989, describes the feet as 'the wings of the heart and also its calendar'. It is a memorable phrase from a meticulous craftsman of the language. It is the journeys on foot one remembers, not the long tedium of the motorway. And it was on foot that I discovered the secret corners of Barcelona and the grandest solitude of the high Pyrenees. I refer to Cela at this point in my own book because he is the author of one of the best travel books about Catalonia – the *Viaje al Pirineo de Lérida* (*Journey to the Lérida Pyrenees*). Perhaps his newly acquired international reputation as a controversial Nobel prizewinner will eventually produce an English translation of this book, full of wit, charm and vitality, a tribute to the survival of the human spirit in the grey days of the Franco dictatorship. The book was of personal interest to me, in that it was written and published between my own first visit to Catalonia, on a school exchange in 1962, and the period during which I lived and worked in Barcelona (1968–70).

Of the small number of other travel books I shall make passing reference to, Rose Macaulay's *Fabled Shore* and Josep Pla's *Costa Brava* predate the development of large-scale tourism on the coast of Catalonia, the part best known to English language readers. I carried both books in my rucksack while walking the northern part of the Costa Brava during the wet, cold Holy Week of 1969. Pla describes each cove in loving and intricate detail, but even in 1969, isolated collections of fishermen's huts had already developed into hotel and apartment resorts. This process has continued, and in chapter 11 I reflect on the impact of tourism, both mass and luxury, on the coast. Macaulay's historical and cultural ponderings, out of fashion as they now probably are, inspired me to write a chapter on the Mediterranean world, and that sense of profound continuity in the Catalan lands which is both intensely strange and attractive to people from the northern and western outposts of Europe. And I have tried to do so in such a way that does not assume the classical, literary heritage that was second nature to Macaulay's generation.

I must also reflect a particular debt to Alistair Boyd, whose book *The Essence of Catalonia*, published in 1988, breaks new ground for the English reader because of its insistence on using the correct Catalan version of place names, rather than their Castilian Spanish equivalents. This, in turn, reflects the change from the centralised state of Franquist Spain to the Spain of the autonomous regions. This process was not inevitable. The Spanish Civil War of 1936–9 had not just been a question of victory by the fascist right over the socialist left. It had also meant the rule of Madrid over Catalans, Basques and Galicians, all of whom have their own language and institutions. In the case of Catalonia it was the massive public demonstrations of 1976 and 1977 that opened the way for a return of the Catalan language to its rightful position as the national language of Catalonia. The Catalan autonomous government has developed a policy of 'linguistic normalisation', which enjoys broad political support and considerable prestige and respect on a European level. I have followed this practice as consistently as possible, although to help the reader who may be more familiar with Castilian versions of names, I have given the Castilian form in brackets where these occur for the first time, e.g. Lleida (Lérida), the inland of the four Spanish provinces that make up modern Catalonia, and Empúries (Ampurias), the hauntingly beautiful Greek and Roman ruins near L'Escala (La Escala). In a very few cases I have given the usual English version, e.g. Mallorca (Majorca), and subsequently used the English version.

As for institutions, I have tried to be as consistent as possible in using English equivalents where there are English equivalents, but to keep to the original Catalan where there is no directly comparable institution. So the reader will find 'town council' for Ajuntament but Generalitat for the autonomous Catalan government.

This is also a good place to make it clear that this is a book about Catalonia, rather than the Catalan-speaking lands, which include Valencia, the Balearic Islands and the French area of Rousillon, as well as the independent principality of Andorra. That would be a more ambitious project, and I prefer to write about what I know best – the four Spanish provinces now seeking to carve out a new future for themselves as autonomous Catalonia.

Vilabertran, 23 July 1990. There are thick-trunked, leafy plane trees outside the monastery and shade in which to park. An apparently dead dog raises its head, sniffs and goes back to sleep. It is a working village, more trucks and tractors than tourists. A trio of kittens scuttle through a wooden gate. The mother remains, ears pricked in the dust. The stones glow golden in the early morning sunshine.

In the Plaça de Catalunya, the main square, are four cars, three vans, one tractor, a tobacconist's, a chemist's, a bank, a savings bank, a telephone kiosk, a café and a fountain; it is a village that takes itself seriously. One house is larger than all the rest, with a round tower and ornamental blue tiles, perhaps built by a Catalan who had made his fortune in Cuba in the nineteenth century and returned home to lord it over his neighbours.

It has taken me thirty minutes to complete my tour of inspection of the village and to arrive back at my shady parking place. An old man sits on a seat, his bike propped against it.

'Bon dia.'

'Bon dia. Do you want to visit the monastery?'

'Yes, I've been waiting. It's open now, isn't it?'

'It's closed on Mondays.'

Of course, I should have known! Most museums close on Mondays, and I've failed again to read the small print. He explains that a young man comes over from Lladó every day to open up. Most days he calls in at the village café for a coffee. My new friend invites me to sit down and share his bench for a while. I do so. He is a republican veteran of the Civil War, wounded in the arm and stomach at the battle of the Ebre River. Until recently he had never received a pension to compensate for his missing finger: only the victors (Franco's forces) received compensation and pensions. He joined the exodus across the border into France, only twenty-five kilometres away, when the war ended in 1939, but was too poor to get to Mexico and real safety. When France was overrun by the Germans he found himself recruited as war labour to a munitions factory in the Pas

xi

de Calais. From there he escaped, crossed France, walked across the Pyrenees and laid low for years in Barcelona. Now he is back home again, as keen to talk about the present as the past:

'I was up at six o'clock this morning to water my garden – peppers and tomatoes. Now I'm having a rest, waiting to see what happens.'

Forty-five metres away is the open stone building, recently restored, that serves as a communal laundry.

'They say that an angel jumped from the top of the church tower, and that a spring of water shot out of the ground on the same spot. That's what they say, but I don't believe them. Do you?'

Only 200 metres away is the motorway that links Catalonia to France and Europe. Along here every summer several million visitors to Spain drive. Many will hurry on south, some will linger. This is a book for people who love to linger, look and listen.

It is an account of one person's contact with a country over a period of thirty years. It is written in the hope that other independent-minded people will feel inspired to travel seeking to understand rather than to judge, and to recognise the ideas and values we share as well as those that distinguish nations one from another.

Chapter 1

Barcelona and Catalonia: City and Country

How do we explain our loves to other people? Either in detail or not at all!

So it is with the city. And like our loves, they find us. I didn't choose to be born and brought up in Bath, especially the dull, provincial, wrong-side-of-the-tracks Bath of the 1950s. But something of the city rubs off, the weekly contact with a great medieval building like Bath Abbey, its being there, its life in stone; the childhood games and picnics in the Royal Victoria Park beside the great crescents and terraces of Georgian Bath. I am sure I acquired a feel for the rational city, the city as the flower of the peaceful arts, of culture and of order in society.

At school in Bath, I was of course exposed to this current of thinking, however little impression it made on me at the time. But looking back on those early lessons about great cities, I am conscious of contradictions between theory and experience, the city as artifact and the city as lived experience. Yes, there were the Royal Crescent and the Circus, the restored and cleaned Abbey, the rebuilt Assembly Rooms rising from the rubble of wartime bombing. But when the wind turned southerly in summer, we had to screw our noses up at the stench from the nearby gasworks, while in winter the mournful echoes of steam engines in the Somerset and Dorset Railway marshalling yards punctuated the noonday pallor. And comfort and splendour were hard to come by. The 'town', as we called it, was a bus ride away, concerts happened in another world and the theatre meant only Christmas pantomimes.

Other writers about the city have sought to redefine the city in terms of modern experience: anonymity, changing roles and identities, secret lives, and a kind of freedom not to be had in either the rational city of the eighteenth century, or the tight-knit community of the village.

1

If it was the anonymity of Barcelona, the desire to sort out my life and build a new identity that prompted me to go and live there for two years from 1968 to 1970, I discovered there another aspect to the city. Living in the heart of the old city, where the stones reverberate with history, it became for me time in reverse. Time, not in the everyday sense of a present that leads inexorably into a future, but a present that refers always to what went before, and a past that refers in turn to its own past, its own becoming, a cumulative quest for origins, for the causes of our semicivilised state. Because we are not truly civilised. We have culture and technology, but we have still not engaged with the ultimate enemy, the paranoid streak of self-destructiveness that is present in every culture and every time. People have invented the city but they are still learning how to use it. The stones of Barcelona still bear the scars of the executioners' bullets from the days of the Spanish Civil War (1936–9).

I have loved Barcelona. It is, in a small way, my world. Its surface is bright, metallic, hard. But beneath that surface lies the real city of dream, imagination and myth. Beyond that particular love is a more general love for Catalonia and its people. Its organised anarchy appeals to something deep within me, an alternative identity that could never grow and flourish in the massive predictability of post-war Bath. And through that love, the coherence of Barcelona and Catalonia, of city and countryside, emerge, the dreams of the past become its present reality and its contradictions are healed by the sweet medicine of imagination.

The beach café at Laredo, Cantabria, 25 April 1990. Beach cafés out of season always end up by asking insistent questions about purpose in life. They offer, too, a consistent answer – that human life is futile, transitory and accidental. Or perhaps it is just the closeness of the sea, because the ancient Greeks, a maritime people, knew that too. Ten days ago I had got quietly drunk on similar feelings at Sant Feliu de Guíxols on the Catalan coast, watching the sea beyond the deserted beach change from palest turquoise to deepest blue and finally to black nothingness. Now the prospect is misty, the deserted beach, the grey sea almost indistinguishable from the grey sky and the hazy mountain dominating the bay. The vastness of the Atlantic and its unknown destinations form a stark contrast to the timeworn intimacy of the Mediterranean.

Beer and olives. The linked tastes of North and South. They're laying for dinner, just in case someone comes. But it doesn't seem very likely. For my part, I have no intention of eating here on my own. I shall lose myself in the dark, noisy bars of the old town. I go across and talk to the waiter who is poking the lobsters and fish in his live tank.

'Does it always rain here?'

'Today's much better. The first time it hasn't rained since Easter!'

'So it does always rain here?'

'Not at all. Before Easter we had fourteen months of drought. It's never happened before.'

Maybe drought, like poverty or hunger, is a relative term in this green, fertile land of hay fields and cattle between the folds of the mountains, just twenty-four hours on the ferry from Plymouth.

The Mediterranean plays a crucial part in the Catalan climate, ensuring mild winters in the coastal area, especially south of Barcelona, and cooling breezes to temper the heat of summer. Rain is most frequent in spring and autumn. Inland the climate is more extreme. Lleida is hot and dry in summer, cold and dry in winter, while the Pyrenees and their foothills collect abundant rain and snow. In spring you can ski in the Pyrenees and sunbathe on the beaches of Tarragona on the same day. The northerly *Tramuntana* wind brings colder weather south from the mountains but seldom penetrates beyond Barcelona. While tourists may prefer the mild coastal areas, Sant Hilari Sacalm, an inland resort 800 metres up in the foothills and home of the popular Font Vella mineral waters, boasts that it has the 'ideal climate': 'Cool temperatures in summer and colder in winter, with plenty of rain and a little snow.'

I reflect on my long day's drive across the open vastness of Northern Spain, from the Mediterranean to the Atlantic. From Vilanova i La Geltrú with its fishing fleet, its Pirelli tyre factory, its lovely golden beaches across the low coastal hills to the motorway. Then on past Lleida (Lérida), the outpost of the Catalan world, on the way to Saragossa. Past Saragossa. Past the signposts indicating the way to the towns and villages of Old

Castile – Soria, Burgos, Santo Domingo de la Calzada on the road to Santiago, which Chaucer's Wife of Bath had travelled. Then a sharp April shower on the tender, budding vines of La Rioja, red dust turning quickly to red mud. La Rioja, wine-rich, modern suburbs of ancient towns, flats and wineries clustering around old, gnarled city centres.

To travel from Mediterranean Spain to Atlantic Spain is to travel through the new, democratic Spain of the autonomous regions – Catalonia, Aragon, the Community of La Rioja, the Community of Rights (or Chartered Community) of Navarre, Euskadi (the Basque Country), Cantabria. A new Spain trying to make good the historical error of a Madrid-focused centralism. Madrid is the highest capital in Europe, and the one with the least history. A new Spain trying to respect and listen to what the great Catalan poet of Franco's Spain, Salvador Espriu, called 'the ways of speaking of her children', ways in which Madrid is a voice among many, rather than always the one voice that insists on being heard.

But Catalonia is more than an administrative convenience for modern Spain. That is a criticism that has been voiced with some reason over (for example) La Rioja or Castile-La Mancha. But it is not true of Catalonia. 'Som i serem', 'We are, and we shall be', is a slogan often repeated in Catalonia. It has a resonance and a truth, but also by its insistence hints at uncertainties and insecurities as to what the future of Catalonia will be. This present book is an attempt both to communicate something of the vitality of Catalonia's past and present, and also to point up some of the unanswered questions. 'What are we?'; 'What shall we be?'; 'Who counts in this "we"?' Unfinished historical business seems of the essence of the 1990s . . .

Catalonia's path through history has been stony and difficult. Greeks, Romans, Visigoths and Arabs all passed this way. The Mediterranean, which laps the shores of Catalonia from Portbou on the French frontier to the last Catalan villages of the Ebre (Ebro) delta, is a world apart, and one which reaches far back into Spain's past, beyond the Arabs, Visigoths and Romans to the first contacts between the civilised peoples of the Eastern

Mediterranean (Phoenicians and Greeks especially) and the primitive peoples of the Iberian peninsula in the fifth century BC.

From about AD 800, Christian counties began to spring up south of the Pyrenees, and in AD 988 the Count of Barcelona broke his ties of vassalage with the French king. Catalonia's 1,000 years of history had begun. In 1137 the crowns of Aragon and Catalonia were united and in the Middle Ages, the Aragonese-Catalan Federation became the centre of a great Mediterranean empire based on sea power, trade and piracy. Then, in 1469, Ferdinand of Aragon married Isabella of Castile. Catalonia became an unhappy member of this new Spanish family, more interested in European wars and American conquests than in the rights and privileges of its smallest province.

Spain turned its back on the Mediterranean world. 1492 was the year Columbus reached America. 1492 was also the year of the expulsion from Spain of the Jews, who had made such a significant, if not always appreciated, contribution to administration, trade, crafts and medicine in medieval Catalonia. In the Middle Ages Catalonia had been a great Mediterranean power. After 1491 Catalonia became a backwater of the great Spanish international empire, the axis of which was now the Atlantic and not the Mediterranean. Yet, in one of those ironies of history, it was the eventual involvement of Catalans in the American trade, from the mid-eighteenth century onwards, which brought Catalonia both material wealth and a new, rich source of cultural ideas which influenced deeply the emergence of Barcelona as the great industrial and commercial centre of the Mediterranean that we know today. Barcelona is not just a great city, not just a Mediterranean city. It is the great city of Catalonia. From this, everything else flows. Like ancient Rome, it has often plundered the material and human wealth of its dependants. Just as I was repeatedly assured that 'Catalonia without Barcelona is nothing', I was equally often assured that 'Barcelona without Catalonia would not exist.'

On a number of occasions, Catalonia allied itself with the enemies of Spain (France, Austria, England, at different times), and in the War of the Spanish Succession this led to disaster: in 1716 the Catalans were forced to accept the *Nueva Planta* (New Deal) Acts, which abolished the institutions of Catalonia and substituted direct rule from Madrid. Liberal new economic measures in the eighteenth century opened the way for the industrialisation of Catalonia in the nineteenth century, and a strong revival of nationalism. Under the Second Spanish Republic (1931–6), Catalonia gained a measure of home rule, but with the defeat of the Republican forces by General Franco in the Spanish Civil War, this was followed by a new wave of repression for the language and institutions of the nation.

Because Barcelona has always been the capital of Catalonia, while Madrid did not acquire the status of capital until the sixteenth century, there is no equivalent in Catalonia to the great cities of Castile with their charters and palaces and spheres of influence. Burgos, Segovia, Salamanca, Toledo, Ávila all have historical, cultural and political identities which have remained scornful of the hegemonic claims of artificial, parvenu Madrid.

Tarragona, Girona (Gerona) and Lleida are all towns with their own peculiar attractions and identities. But their subordination to Barcelona is never in doubt. In the late 1960s, I used to go often from Barcelona to Tarragona for quiet weekends by the sea or up-country among the vines and olives and monasteries of 'New Catalonia'. But it was always dull and provincial compared with Barcelona, where the cafés, concert halls, cinemas and theatres were always full, where business, industry and the university were located. Its most talented daughters and sons were often occupied in Barcelona during the week and came home at the weekend for the more homely and modest life style. Then, come Sunday night, they would be crowding round the ticket office at the railway station, hoping for tickets on the Madrid-Barcelona Talgo as the only alternative to the hot, slow, bumpy train known affectionately by one and all as the *Tortuga de Tortosa*, the Tortosa Tortoise.

The operation of the principle of primogeniture has had a profound effect on Catalan society. Rural property has been passed on entire, and younger sons (and more recently daughters) packed off to Barcelona to swell the ranks of the liberal professions – the law, medicine, the civil service – or, in more humble families, to provide the apprentices of the Barcelona craft guilds. It is still the case that few Catalans who live in Barcelona cannot claim some family relationship with a more rural town or village, a tendency encouraged in more recent years as tourism has developed, second homes and holiday apartments have become more common, and the network of rail and road links has become more thoroughly developed. At its most mundane level, the difficulties associated with either leaving the city on a Friday evening or getting back into it on a Sunday evening are eloquent testimony to the ways in which Barcelona is tied into its Catalan identity. The extended family is still very much part of Catalan life, and many people continue to identify strongly with the place they come from rather than the place they happen to work in.

At the same time, to underline the pre-eminence of Barcelona as a feature of Catalan identity is also to see the Catalan nation in the context of widening horizons and changing patterns of population. Since the late nineteenth century, Barcelona has been a major destination for emigration from the poor rural areas of Spain, first of all from Murcia, later from other parts of Andalucía (Andalusia) and from the remoter parts of Extremadura and Galicia. Towards the end of the book, I shall take issue with those who assert that the Catalan nation can only be understood in terms of its older, Catalan-speaking inhabitants. Any attempt to carve out a place for Catalonia in modern Europe must take account of, and include, people of a different linguistic and cultural heritage, as well as more recent arrivals from North Africa and from other parts of Europe. 'Catalonia for the Catalans' is not a respectable political slogan, but it reflects a view that is frequently aired in private. It would be a mean-minded and short-sighted policy to see Catalonia into the twenty-first century.

So Catalonia is a Mediterranean nation and lives with and from its capital, Barcelona. A third feature that distinguishes Catalonia very clearly from other parts of Spain is the fertility of its lands and the denseness of its population. Travelling in the reverse direction from the ferry port at Santander, I arrived in early April 1990 in Lleida. As I turned off the motorway to enter the city, the sky darkened, the air filled with rain, and it fell in a torrential downpour. It was over almost before it had started, but left a twilight of rich beauty. Earth after rain – the elemental smell of the good earth, and the apples and pears in blossom in the orchards of Lleida! And a sign indicated that 'Six million Catalans welcome you.'

Yet, with its alternating pattern of dry and irrigated lands, Lleida is the only part of Catalonia which even begins to suggest the barrenness of so much of central Spain, the monotony of rock-strewn hillsides broken only by the green stains of the great rivers – the Ebro, the Duero, the Guadalquivir. On the road from Saragossa to Lleida, there is a stretch of some 130 kilometres where the only view north from the almost deserted motorway is of the lorries obstinately trundling along the NII main road, refusing to pay the relatively high motorway tolls, and the completely barren hills of the Monegros. In all this distance there cannot be more than four or five settlements which rank above the level of hamlet. By contrast, on the long, straight roads across the green Empordà (Ampurdán) region between Girona and the Costa Brava, there is no point at which you are out of sight of a red-brown village clustered around its medieval parish church, with the large rambling *masies* (farmhouses, originally designed for owners, workers and animals to share) dotted between fields of maize and sunflowers. As Lluís Llach, a modern troubadour from the Empordà, puts it in his song 'País petit' ('Small country'):

> El meu país és tan petit
> que des de dalt d'un campanar
> sempre es pot veure el campanar veí.
> Diuen que els poblets tenen por,
> tenen por de sentir-se sols,
> tenen por de ser massa grans.

(My country is so small / that from the top of one church tower / you can always see the next church tower./ They say the villages are afraid, / afraid of being alone, / afraid of growing too big.)

The distances between the four provincial capitals are also relatively small compared with other parts of the Iberian peninsula. From Barcelona it is only ninety-five kilometres to Tarragona, one hundred and sixty kilometres to Lleida and ninety-five kilometres to Girona.

It is a land rich in material ways, but also rich in people and history and beauty. To paint a picture of Catalonia in terms of its Mediterranean heritage, the interplay of Barcelona and the rest of the country, and the wealth of its lands and peoples, is to draw the picture too broadly, too impressionistically. It is, as I say, the detail that counts, that sum of moments of illumination, human individuals and places which makes up the experience of being in, and part of, a country.

Chapter 2

A Nation Apart?

On the main road from Lleida to Barcelona is the small town of Cervera. This is an attractive part of Catalonia, outside the irrigated fruit orchards of Lleida, but surrounded by olive groves, almond trees and (in spring) green fields. The houses cluster together in hilltop villages for protection. This is partly because this part of Catalonia was, from the ninth to the twelfth century, a war zone, fought over by Christians and Arabs, but partly too because water is in short supply and villages have usually relied on what may be the only well for miles around. The main road from Barcelona to Lleida plunges into a tunnel beneath the hill on which Cervera is set. For many motorists a glimpse of its medieval walls or a church tower in their rear-view mirror is all that the town amounts to.

On the Barcelona side of Cervera, the restoration of the old town walls shows that from the medieval period the town had a certain status. But there is nothing to prepare you for the monstrous grandeur of the old university building which dominates the heart of the town. It was erected between 1718 and 1740 in the grand classical manner, its massive buildings articulated around two courtyards. Part of it is used as a school, but most of it is empty, and as I wander through the courtyards at lunch time, children are playing football and volleyball where once the students must have discussed philosophy, medicine, the state of the Catalan nation, or whatever else eighteenth-century students discussed. Other corners of the stiff, rectangular buildings are being used for an Institut Français and a study centre of the Universidad Nacional de Educación a Distancia, Spain's Open University. But of students or lecturers there is no sign. Only the late baroque façade of the main entrance shows any sense of intellectual liveliness.

To understand the rise and fall of Cervera's university, a brief

9

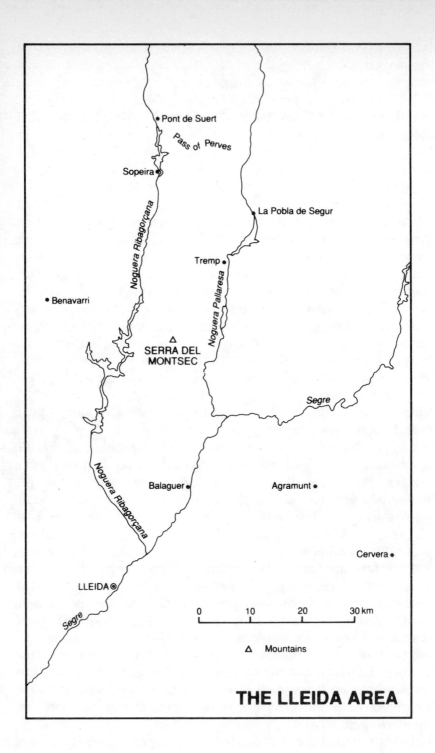

Pont de Suert

Pass of Perves

Sopeira

La Pobla de Segur

Noguera Ribagorçana

Tremp

Noguera Pallaresa

Benavarri

△
SERRA DEL
MONTSEC

Segre

Noguera Ribagorçana

Balaguer

Agramunt

Cervera

LLEIDA

Segre

0   10   20   30 km

△   Mountains

THE LLEIDA AREA

excursion into Catalan history is required. Three times Cervera. has played a key role in the institutional life of Catalonia. It was here in 1359, in a house on the *carrer major* (high street) that the *corts* (the Catalan parliament) agreed to establish the Generalitat, the named used to this day for the Catalan government, a civil power intended to balance the power of the monarch. Then, in 1469, a marriage contract between Ferdinand of Aragon and Isabella of Castile was signed here which led to the union of the two great Spanish kingdoms, Aragon-Catalonia and Castile. Although Catalan customs and practices were maintained, it was the beginning of a slow end for the idea of a separate Catalan state. The climax came in 1700, when a dispute over the succession to the Spanish throne led to the Catalans supporting the Archduke Charles of Austria against the French candidate, the grandson of Louis xv who was eventually to become Philip v of Spain. The Catalans were joining an alliance of England, Holland and Austria which was designed to limit Bourbon power. But the alliance fell apart in 1711 when Charles was recalled to Vienna to succeed as Austrian Emperor. Neither English nor Dutch wanted too close a partnership between Spain and Austria any more than they wanted Spain and France to become too close. Philip seized his opportunity and dealt swiftly and ruthlessly with the Catalans. Military rule was imposed, with a whole swathe of Barcelona demolished to build the fortress (now park) of the Cuitadella. The Catalan language was banned from official use. The liberties and institutions of the Catalans were systematically denied and dismantled. Among these were the Catalan universities of Barcelona and Lleida.

Philip's next move was to build the new university in the politically quiet atmosphere of Cervera. From 1726 until 1842 it was the only university in Catalonia. In retrospect, it is like so many great monuments, nothing more than that, a symbol in stone of a certain ideal of society which appeared monolithic and all-conquering in its day, but which held the seeds of its own destruction. New forces were already stirring which were to overwhelm the old absolutist regimes of eighteenth-century Europe. If France was never the same after the French Revolution, neither was Spain. It was in Cadiz in 1812 that the first liberal constitution in Europe was agreed. Nineteenth-century Spain swayed between monarchy and republic, between liberals and conservatives, but state power was never as secure and

11

monolithic as it had been in the eighteenth century. As for the Catalans, the nineteenth century saw the gradual revival of the Catalan language and literature, the movement known as the *Renaixença* (Renaissance). As part of this process, Barcelona University was reopened in 1842, and the faculties at Cervera moved back to the heart of the Catalan world from their curious outpost on the plains of Catalonia.

The next stage in the story leads inevitably to the frontier, the frontier between France and Spain, and first to the quaint oddity of Colera. This is not a book about camp sites. Yet I must mention the one at Colera. It is in the village, the village is at the seaside. But between the village and its camp site and the sea is an enormous iron railway viaduct which carries the railway between two high cliff tunnels on its way to France. It rises on stone pillars above the dry, stony river bed and the clustered red tiled roofs of the village, dwarfing everything in sight. During the Second Spanish Republic of 1931–6, Catalonia obtained, for the first time since 1714, a measure of autonomy, with the Generalitat restored to its proper place as the supreme political authority. But this in turn was challenged by the military rebellion of Francisco Franco, which led to one of the bloodiest civil wars in European history (1936–9). Franco's fascists made repeated attempts to blow up the bridge but always failed. They destroyed most of the houses in the village but not the bridge.

I was unlucky at Colera, having brought with me a dose of salmonella. It is not the quietest place in Catalonia to spend the night, and between freight trains rumbling across the viaduct and stomach cramps, the camp site took on a nightmare quality. But like the bridge I survived to tell the story. Another survivor (of the fascist bombing) is the spreading, hybrid plane tree with its massive, thick, short trunk in the Plaça Pi i Margall. It almost fills the square with its luxurious greenery, and creates a shady terrace area for the local café.

From Colera, I risked the only road in Catalonia which still gives me bad dreams, the switchback climb across the scrubby headland to Portbou, with its frontier station and fishing port. It tries hard to look like a holiday resort, with its cheerful fishing and pleasure harbour divided by a neat line of buoys from the swimming beach. But it fails. Young, blond men from northern Europe sit drinking excessively large beers at the pavement cafés. French and German are as common at four o'clock in the afternoon as Catalan and

Spanish. And all the time, the cars climb slowly up the next scrubby, maquis-covered hill to the road frontier.

The purpose of my visit to Portbou was to call on some friends, a Barcelona couple who had come up to spend the weekend with the woman's parents. Four generations of the family were gathered in Portbou that weekend. Catalan families remain strong, but the extended family has been a reflection of housing shortages and poverty as well as family ties. The generations remain closer to one another than in the countries of northern Europe. However, comfortable and well appointed old people's homes and centres have appeared all over Catalonia in recent years and reflect the desire of older people to spend time with friends of their own generation as well as with younger members of their own families.

Xavier's father-in-law takes us out in a little old fishing boat with a spluttering outboard motor. We look down at the mussel and oyster beds which lie at the foot of the cliffs and swim in the deep clear waters of the bay, Xavier dark haired with smooth, brown skin, his daughter all pink and golden, the two extremes of Catalan physical characteristics. The father-in-law, a Barcelona lawyer, a tall greying patriarch of a man, tells me the story of the boat: it was built as a fishing boat by his grandfather in 1931, was requisitioned for republican coastguard duties during the Civil War; at the end of the war, with the remnants of the republic fleeing across the border to safety in France (at least until the Nazis arrived), it disappeared. Several years later it was found abandoned on a rocky beach down the coast, returned to Portbou, and has since been used as a family pleasure boat. As we chug back towards the harbour in the dusk, Portbou is a work of art, the rounded contours of the hills behind which the sun has already set, the cuboid houses looped around the horse-shoe-shaped bay.

This is a land of exile and escape. Just across the border at Port Vendres in France, the Glaswegian architect of the Glasgow School of Art, Charles Rennie McIntosh, turned to painting as a compensation for what he saw as the failure of the British Establishment to recognise his architectural genius. McIntosh went home to die. One exile who didn't was the German philosopher, Walter Benjamin. He reached Portbou in 1940, fleeing south from the Nazis. His journey ended at Portbou with suicide in an anonymous hotel bedroom. Hope had evaporated behind him, and there was no hope to be had in Franco's Spain. He is buried in the cemetery on the hillside above the village. As

13

for me, I have crossed and re-crossed the border at Portbou many times, a failed exile become an unrepentant traveller. I was employed to teach English at the University of Barcelona. But under Franco's rules, the university as a state institution was not allowed to employ foreigners. I was therefore unable to obtain a work or residence permit. The only solution was to cross the border every three months, get my passport stamped and come back a few days later. Life was like that in Franco's Spain.

Talking openly to older people in Catalonia is a useful reminder of how jagged and uneven the path of European history is. The final stage in this three-part tale of Catalonia's efforts striving towards nationhood, its historical 'will to exist' as the Conservative Nationalists who run the Generalitat today call it, takes place on 23 April 1990, St George's Day. Saint George is the patron saint not just of England, but of Genoa and Catalonia and countless other places as well. He is one of the Church's most popular, if maverick, saints, the helper of maidens in distress and more generally the weak against the strong. Maidens in distress may well have learned to look after themselves but the poor and weak are always with us.

The cult of St George took root in England, Barcelona and Genoa at a period in the Middle Ages when each was establishing a commercial empire for itself. It is as if they needed a view of themselves as small and vulnerable nations to justify their expansionist tendencies. The enemies of England, Genoa and Catalonia may have had far more need of the protection of this chivalrous saint.

Since the fifteenth century, the giving of roses by men to the women they love has been part of the folklore of Sant Jordi. During the Franco years, the red rose was also an eloquent political statement in a land where politics was banned, and year after year the streets of Catalan towns were filled with stalls selling roses – and books. Because more recently something else has been added – the national book day, for 23 April is also the birthday of both Shakespeare and Cervantes, his great Spanish contemporary. A crowd has gathered outside a bookshop in one of Europe's loveliest streets, the Passeig de Gràcia (Paseo de Gracia) in Barcelona. An elderly man on a second-floor balcony, in a bow tie and a grey suit which hangs loosely from his gaunt, tired limbs, gazes down at the crowd outside the bookshop. A stall has been set up on the pavement, but as I emerge by chance from the railway station beneath, the murmur goes round the crowd that a very special visitor is expected. That visitor is Prince Philip, Bourbon heir to the Spanish throne, who has come to Catalonia to meet the people, and to take possession of his territories, a little as Prince Charles once went to Caernarfon to be invested as Prince of Wales.

The new Spanish royal family is low-key and democratic. It is one of the cheapest royal families to maintain in Europe (Britain's is one of the most expensive). The story of how Juan Carlos, the present Bourbon King of Spain, gained his throne is unlikely in the extreme. When Franco decided that eventually the monarchy would return to Spain, he picked not the claimant to the throne (Juan de Borbón, Count of Barcelona) but his son, Juan Carlos. Little is known about the life of this rather lonely figure, trained for the crown in the shadow of an ageing dictator. No doubt Franco hoped that many of the characteristics of his own long period of rule would be kept up by the new King – the privileged position of the Catholic Church and the army, censorship, limited political rights. In the event, Juan Carlos moved swiftly in the years after 1975 to ensure the full return to democracy in Spain. Any lingering doubts people may have had about his commitment to democracy were put aside after the events of '23F', 23 February 1981, when a Civil Guard took over at gunpoint the parliament in Madrid. It was the personal intervention of the King in a stream of phone calls that secured the loyalty of the army to the new Spain rather than the tired old illusions of the extreme right.

So here was a prince in the Passeig de Gràcia buying his books with cash from his own pocket, swapping jokes with the shop assistants, surrounded, not by the pomp of Church and army, but by a posse of plain-clothes bodyguards in their dark, plain-clothes bodyguard suits. A half-smile threatens the expressionless face of the elderly viewer on the second-floor balcony. It is his only comment. I wondered if he had been looking down during the great pro-autonomy demonstrations of 1976 and 1977, or when the nationalist army rolled into town with their tanks in 1939, or when the people's militias, socialists, Trotskyites, communists, anarchists marched past in 1936 on their way to the front to fight for democracy.

The immediate scene before me was dominated by three men. Alongside the Prince was Jordi Pujol, President of the Generalitat, the Catalan autonomous government. Pujol and the Prince, seen everywhere together that April week, made an astonishing pair, the Prince tall as an American college basketball player, lean, young and fit; Pujol, a short, rotund little man, balding on top, looking tired and past his prime. Prince Philip, a man born to be king and being constantly groomed in public affairs; Pujol, whose politics were forged in clandestine opposition to the Franco regime. Don Quixote and Sancho Panza, I thought, and my book had suddenly acquired a working title: *The land of the tall, thin prince and the short, fat president.* And then the third man, Pasqual Maragall, the handsome Mayor of Barcelona and prospective host of the 1992 Olympic Games. Tall and well-built with steel-grey hair and dark moustache, he is a dark-suited socialist of the new European variety, cheerfully aware of the political advantage to be gained from a public appearance at the side of Pujol, his main political enemy from across the other side of the Plaça Sant Jaume, where socialist town hall and nationalist Generalitat confront one another at all hours of night and day.

Catalan autonomy now exists within the context of a monarchy rather than a republic, and this is a crucial difference between Catalonia in the 1930s and 1990s. The new king is a Bourbon. Bourbons are little loved in Catalonia, yet he is accepted. Despite their historical crime of dismantling Catalan institutions in the eighteenth century, the Bourbons can be seen in retrospect as a modernising influence on Spain. They encouraged the growth of trade and industry in Catalonia, and by permitting Catalans to take part in the American trade from which they had been excluded by the monopoly granted by the Spanish crown to Seville, they gave Catalonia an economic and cultural life that was to be of vital importance in the growth of nineteenth-century Catalonia as an industrial power. In the unforgettable words of Santiago Carrillo, the elderly leader of the Spanish Communist Party at the time, 'Better a possible monarchy than an impossible republic.' At a Sant Jordi party in Barcelona during the Prince's visit, I found few people prepared to criticise the monarchy, and a general acceptance that it offered a point of stability in the changing world of modern Spain, a point of reference in the uncharted waters of decentralisation.

'You English have a democracy and a queen. Why should we Catalans not have a democracy and a king?'

'But British democracy doesn't depend on the Queen!'

'For us, the King is a necessity.'

Indeed, the sympathetic attitude of Prince Philip was contrasted favourably with what was seen as the continuing disregard for Catalan sensibilities of the Spanish socialist Prime Minister, Felipe González, whose main power base has always been Seville. 'Your language is also my language,' the young Prince announced to an enraptured Catalan parliament, speaking in both Castilian and Catalan. The emotional impact was the equivalent of John F. Kennedy going to Berlin to announce, 'Ich bin ein Berliner.'

Another element of continuity is the continuing strength of Catalan industry and commerce. New industries have been attracted here, in particular from Germany and Japan, to follow the influx of American firms in the 1960s and 1970s. Pujol has visited Tokyo on a number of occasions and claims the Japanese and Catalans have a considerable affinity. Some Catalan industry has been in decline, noticeably textiles, the basis of Catalonia's industrial revolution. However, this is not, of course, an exclusively Catalan experience, but one shared in Western Europe in the face of lower labour costs in South and East Asia. There is some reason to think, too, that the high rates of unemployment in Spain, the highest in the European Community, are somewhat cushioned by the mutual support of members of the extended family. In general, affluence is apparent on the streets, in the well-stocked shops, large apartment stores and trendy boutiques of towns such as Barcelona and Lleida. Poverty is something to be kept at home, and the lunch-time and evening promenades, when people can show off their own fashionable clothes, beautifully dressed babies and children, have never been more popular. The Catalans are good at making money, and good at spending it, too. I often felt under-dressed in design-conscious Barcelona in my comfortable, casual London clothes.

Modernisation of industry has been supported by modernisation on the land. The peasant farmer collecting the first hay harvest in his horse and cart, which was one of the first things I saw on leaving the ferry port at Santander in northern Spain, would certainly have raised eyebrows in Catalonia, where agriculture has long been mechanised. Irrigation is the key to the success of Catalan agriculture, especially on the fruit-growing plains around Lleida and in the delta of the Ebre, where rice is the main crop. Even where farming goes on in a more leisurely,

17

traditional way, in the high valleys of the Pyrenees, where the animals share the farmhouse in winter and go off to the high alpine meadows in summer, there is an air of relative affluence. Catalonia no longer feels like a peasant society.

With its continuing industrial importance goes the continuing importance of immigration, especially in Barcelona and the surrounding towns, where three-quarters of the population of Catalonia live. This was also an important force in the 1920s and 1930s, when hundreds of thousands of peasants left the land in Murcia and other parts of Andalusia to look for jobs in the industrial centres of Catalonia and the Basque Country. This created a problem of cultural and national identity. In the 1950s and 1960s, Andalusian immigration continued with other flows coming from the poor, dry lands of Extremadura on the Portuguese frontier, and from backward, rural Galicia. There are immigrants, too, from North Africa, and of course with foreign investment and EC membership have come substantial numbers of other Europeans. Barcelona is a melting-pot, as it always has been.

Catalan politics have changed as well, one major difference being the decline of the politics of the outside left. In particular, anarchism, a political movement which attracted much support from both the native Catalan and immigrant working class in the 1930s, is now a spent force. So too is POUM, the Trotskyite party in whose militias George Orwell was unfortunate enough to enrol during the Spanish war. If he had made a different choice, *Homage to Catalonia* might have been more about the conflict between fascism and democracy and less about communists and Trotskyites fighting their own dirty little war within a war. There is still interest in Orwell in Catalonia, but also some puzzlement as to why he chose to base his rejection of Russian-style communism on what happened in the streets of Barcelona in 1937 rather than on what Stalin was doing back in Russia in the 1930s, or as John Langdon-Davies did, on the cynical Stalin-Hitler non-aggression pact of 1939. Pierre Vilar has written in his monumental history of Catalonia, published in 1987: 'I do not believe that Orwell understood very much about the meaning of the struggle he had wanted to take part in.'

The dominant party in Catalonia is now Pujol's own Convergència Democràtica de Catalunya (CDC), which has governed since the first autonomous election in a generally happy coalition with Unió Democràtica de Catalunya under the combined title Convergència i Unió (CiU). Convergence and union! How well it expresses Pujol's own personal aim to be the dominant force in Catalan politics and to identify the cause of Catalonia with his own person. His own personal status owes much to having been tortured and imprisoned in the repression which followed Franco's visit to Barcelona in 1960. The Orfeó Català, Catalonia's best-known choir, was due to sing at a concert in the rich, art nouveau setting of the Catalan Palace of Music (the Palau for short). At the last moment, a song with words by Catalonia's best-loved poet, Joan Maragall, was excluded from the programme by Franco's Civil Governor. This led to a well-organised protest at the concert, with the audience clamouring for the piece to be played and attempting to sing it themselves. Such is the power of language and culture in the Catalan nation! Pujol was arrested as the ringleader, tortured and sentenced to seven years for military rebellion, of which he spent two years in Saragossa jail and six months confined to Girona. The Pujol who emerged was a different man from the young Catholic social democrat of the 1950s student movement. Pujol now devoted himself to *fer país* (to build up the country), using his family connections to build a business empire and increasingly identifying the future of Catalonia with an unregulated neo-liberal economic policy. Former colleagues in the CC (Crist i Catalunya) movement, who were developing towards the left in response to influences such as Pope John xxiii, the Vatican Council, liberation theology and the worker-priest movement, were now described by him as 'incoherent and confusing'. And another word – *Lerrouxist*.

To understand the force of the word *Lerrouxist* in Catalan politics, it is necessary to take another small step backwards to the turn of the century and the republican party organised by the anti-Catalan demagogue, Alejandro Lerroux. His following was especially strong among the early waves of immigrants, and ever since then his name has been used as a pejorative term for any Catalan politician who dares to put the Spanish dimension of politics before the Catalan dimension. It is especially effective when used by Pujol, who has always claimed to some extent to stand above politics, a national martyr and nation builder. This claim is only true in part, though, and Pujol's political success contrasts starkly with the muddied waters surrounding the collapse of his Banca Catalana banking empire. As several people

19

told me, they would rather trust Pujol with the Generalitat than with their savings. Another senior member of his own party told me the standard joke that although Sant Jordi (Saint George) is the patron saint of Catalonia, the Catalans have never had a King Jordi – until now.

It is the force of the term *Lerrouxist* which has made life especially difficult for the Catalan Socialist Party (PSC), which contests elections under the joint banner of PSC-PSOE with González's Spanish Socialist Workers Party. Since PSOE rules in Madrid and Catalan nationalism feeds on resentment of Madrid and all its works, the PSC is then caught on the horns of a dilemma: the PSC-PSOE link gives it credibility and power in Madrid, but actually loses it votes at home in the autonomous elections. The position is very similar in the Basque Country, where the neo-conservative Basque Nationalist Party rules. The compensation for the socialists is their control over the Barcelona City Council, where Maragall is as powerful a figure as Pujol at the Generalitat. The socialists hope that the high profile of Barcelona and its mayor before and during the 1992 Olympics will eventually sweep them to power in the Generalitat. In any case, there is little evidence of a revival of *Lerrouxism* in Catalonia. Mass immigration ceased in 1975, and there was an actual net loss of population between 1981 and 1986. Most of the non-Catalan population are second generation immigrants born in Catalonia, and particularly as the use of Catalan as the normal language of education works its way through the school system, are likely to identify themselves as Catalans rather than Andalusians or Galicians.

To see that there is no reason why being a good Catalan cannot include being a good Spaniard, or European, or internationalist, it is good to travel down to El Vendrell, on the fringes of the lands of Tarragona. In the best traveller's tradition, I came upon it by accident while trying to avoid a traffic jam in Vendrell itself. Here, in the coastal suburb of Sant Salvador, is the house of Pau Casals, cellist and statesman. A neat little row of period houses give straight onto the beach, some of them dating back to the nineteenth century when Sant Salvador was an important port for the export of wine and spirits to America. The Casals house is surrounded by a lovely garden heady with the scent of pines and the sighing of the sea breeze in the palms. From the open walkway above the gallery a view opens up of the beach both

20

ways, with little boats drawn up on the sand. Fine statues ornament the garden, too, with lemon trees, pelargoniums in flower, succulents and flowerbeds surrounded by neat little hedges of sweet-smelling Mediterranean herbs. Inside the house, the curator puts on Rodrigo's *Concierto de Aranjuez* to welcome me. Art and life, nature and art, land and sea, culture and politics, this little museum makes these links in the most effective way possible, drawn as it is around the life of one extraordinary but representative man who remained loyal to Catalonia and to the Spanish Republic in defeat, explaining: 'I never forget my humble birth and I will always stand by my fellow countrymen.' To emphasise his attachment to Catalonia, his long exile, lasting until his death, was centred on Prada de Conflent (Prades, in French) in the foothills of the Pyrenees on the French side of the border.

Casals became the epitome of the international artist, the world citizen who also acknowledged his roots and his indebtedness to a particular cultural heritage. As early as 1927 a street had been named after him in his home town of El Vendrell, an event celebrated by an open-air concert. Working-class men crowded around to listen to Casals and his orchestra. At an official Generalitat concert at the Montjuïc palace in 1932, the first part was devoted to *sardanas* (a Catalan folk dance) played by a traditional *cobla* band. In the second part, local choirs joined forces for Beethoven's Ninth Symphony, and in the third part the Orfeó Català performed songs, including their conductor Millet's arrangement of a traditional song *'El Cant dels Ocells'* ('Birdsong'). In later years the arrangement for solo cello was to become an integral part of every Casals concert as an expression of devotion to the homeland.

In the sitting room of the house is a glass cabinet containing a collection of locally carved figures for the crib, that distinctive Catalan tradition which can be seen in every church and many shops and private houses in the weeks before Christmas. Here is the inspiration, then, for Casals' great peace anthem, the oratorio *El Pessebre The Crib*, which was performed all over the world from 1960, including Berlin, London and the United Nations in New York as part of the celebrations of the fifteenth anniversary of the Universal Declaration of Human Rights. In a message to the United Nations in 1958 he had said: 'I used music and my voice to draw attention to the suffering which afflicts mankind because of the great and perhaps mortal danger of nuclear weapons threatening us. Music, that universal language which is understood by everyone, should be a source of communication among men.' Yet the final room returns the visitor to Catalonia itself and a Catalan tile showing the Virgin of Montserrat, Catalonia's national shrine, and the words:

> Dolça Catalunya
> Patria del meu cor
> quan de tu s'allunya
> d'enyorança es mor

(Sweet Catalonia, land of my heart, whoever leaves you will die of home-sickness.)

Casals died at the age of ninety-six as he had lived for thirty-four years – an exile. His remains were brought home to Catalonia in November 1979.

Chapter 3

The Mediterranean World

The sea is a permanent part of Catalonia. In the garden of Pau Casals' house at Sant Salvador you hear the eternal murmur of the Mediterranean sea on the sandy beach. Each of the eight wind directions has its own name, and these names – *Tramuntana, Gregal, Levant, Xaloc, Migjorn, Garbí, Ponent, Mestral* (from north clockwise) – are not historical anachronisms but still part of the everyday experience and language of the people. 'The *Tramuntana* is blowing today', I was told at a petrol station on a bitterly cold April day in the Empordà, with every bit of mist and pollution blown away and the fresh snow on the Pyrenees seeming so close you could stretch out and touch it. Medieval Catalan poetry is full of the winds, which relate to the adventures of the medieval Catalan pirates, but also have a symbolic value. They represent something of the chance nature of human life. A sudden storm blows up from nowhere in the treacherous waters between Spain and Italy, a ship is sunk, lives are lost. This has no sense or reason unless you assume that that is indeed the law of life and fate.

To the certainty of death is added the uncertainty of love. In one poem, Ausiàs March, a Valencian-born poet of the first half of the fifteenth century, wrote:

> Amor, de vós io sent més que no en sé
> de que la part pijor me'n romandrà;
> e de vós sap lo qui sens vós està.
> A joc de daus vos acompararé.

(Love, I sense rather than know about you / that my share will be the worst part, / and those who are without you know you too. / I shall compare you to a game of dice.)

GIRONA AND THE COSTA BRAVA

Scale: 0 10 20 30 km

Legend:
- —·—·— International boundary
- △ Mountains
- ✛ Monastery
- □ Greco-Roman remains

△ CANIGÓ

FRANCE

Port Vendres

La Jonquera

Portbou
Colera

El Port de la Selva
Sant Pere de Rodes

CAP DE CREUS

Cadaqués

Vilabertran
Figueres
Castelló d' Empúries

Roses

EMPORDÀ

Besalú
Fluvià

Aiguamolls de L'Empordà Natural Park

GARROTXA

Olot

Empúries
L'Escala

△ FINESTRES

Llemena
Brugent

Ter

△ ROCACORBA

L'Estartit

Islas Medes Natural Park

Ter

◉ GIRONA

Peratallada
La Bisbal

Pals
Begur
Aiguablava

● Sant Hilari Sacalm

△ SERRA DE MONTSENY

Sant Feliu de Guíxols

COSTA BRAVA

Tossa

Lloret

Blanes

MEDITERRANEAN SEA

24

This poem ('Veles e vents', 'Sails and winds') became very well known in the late 1960s in a sung version by Raimon, also Valencian born, and one of the finest folk singers to emerge in Catalonia in recent years. In its original form, the poem shows a profound pessimism as well as keen insights into the psychology of love. The very recovery of the Catalan past was a political statement in the difficult conditions of censorship and repression in the late 1960s and early 1970s. So his love song is a political statement as much as 'Sobre la pau' ('Peace song'):

> De vegades la pau
> és com un desert
> sense veus ni arbres
> com un buit inmens on moren els homes.

(Sometimes peace / is like a desert / without voices or trees / like an immense void where people are dying.)

El mar, la mar – the sea is very special in both Spanish and Catalan in being one of a tiny number of nouns which can be both masculine and feminine. It represents the unity of the world but also its duality. The masculine and feminine principles. Two of the sculptures in the garden at Sant Salvador are outstanding. Both are nudes. One is an Apollo by Josep Clarà (1878–1958), the other a woman by Josep Llimona (1864–1934). How easily the mind slips in time and place, to the ancient world of Greece and Rome, and then back again to the present and this peaceful garden in the still warmth of a spring afternoon.

The past in Catalonia is always present. And nowhere more so than in Tarragona. Driving down the coast road a few days after my visit to Sant Salvador felt like a homecoming. Even in winter, Tarragona is always warmer and sunnier than Barcelona, and little wonder that the Romans chose it as their winter head-quarters. Soon, the familiar signs appear. First the Arc de Berà, a Roman triumphal arch erected on the great Roman Via Augusta, the highway of imperial Roman Catalonia. Built by one of the Emperor Trajan's generals between AD 98 and 117, it continued to span, until very recently, the main road from Barcelona to Tarragona. Now the road skirts it on both sides, and it is easy to stop and admire the immense archway with its Corinthian pillars. A little further towards Tarragona, and again right on the main road, is Scipio's tower, built of great blocks of local stone. The only thing known for certain is that it appears to have no connection with the Scipio brothers! But such is the force of local legend that it is unlikely that it will ever be called anything else, for it was Scipio who originally established Tarraco as a military base in 218 BC against the troublesome tribes of the interior who supported the Carthaginians in the Punic wars.

The Romans ruled Spain for 600 years, and their Empire provided not just political unity but also the cultural and linguistic unity of the Latin language. Until recently, the use of Latin was preserved by the 'universal' Catholic Church, but of course the everyday Latin spoken by the peoples of the Roman Empire was never identical from one part to another. In Spain, this was to give rise eventually to the emergence of Portuguese, Castilian and Catalan as separate languages.

Then the long view of the beach, the ships moving in and out of the busy commercial port to the left, and on the right the heart of the Roman-medieval city on the hill. Tarragona of the golden light on ancient golden stone, the morning sun slanting in across a glittering silver sea, touching everything, a time warp of a city.

The place that most immediately puts you in touch with the life of the city, as in most Catalan towns, is the *rambla*, the broad road with its central pedestrian walkway, which slopes slightly upwards towards the sea. Perhaps it is this sloping to the sea on a due north-south axis that helps to give the *rambla* its special quality of light, a luminosity, an absence of shadows, and yet also oblique as if caressing everything it touches. On its south side are banks and savings banks, on its north side shops and cafés and a fine brick *modernista* (loosely, art nouveau, though the term will later be explained fully) school. Broad and orderly, it initially seems grander yet more intimate than Barcelona's better-known *rambla*, a gorge between the high buildings of the old town, with narrow streets opening off on both sides. On the other hand, Barcelona's *rambla* is filled with tourists, sailors, visitors from all over the world, while Tarragona's *rambla* is more intimate, even provincial, in that special sense of being a place where, by and large, people still know one another. In Barcelona, a meeting by chance in the street with a friend is an unusual occurrence.

Since I knew Tarragona in the 1960s little has changed in the *rambla*. The *modernista* façades have been cleaned and restored to their 1900s glory. There are, too, newcomers, most noticeably the offices of trade unions and political parties, and a lot more bookshops. The bookshops themselves are a reflection of Tarragona's self-consciousness as an ancient city, full of esoteric monographs on the past as well as a newer generation of more popular volumes on local history. This is a city to pause and browse and ponder in.

Tarragona, despite its Gothic cathedral, is not dark and medieval. The old nucleus of the town is surrounded and defined by the Roman walls of which more than a kilometre are clearly visible. The lower portion and the gateway surrounds are made from huge megalithic blocks, always referred to as Cyclopean, such is their legendary size and appearance. There are sections where the walls stand solemn and imposing and alone. I prefer the area around the Sant Antoni gate, where Roman, medieval and modern mingle in wild abandon. The gateway itself was rebuilt in 1757, and gives access from the old city to an open play area for children, with an old people's centre on one side, the drop to the sea on another and a backdrop of houses built directly onto and above the Roman walls. Even in April, the midday sun is hot after the cool streets of the old town. When I first took a photo of this doorway, I was looking at it as an isolated artistic event, but now I see it as summing up that flow and continuity of the city – not least when a local bus suddenly squeezes through it. From here, heading back towards the *rambla*, you follow a dusty, mimosa-lined little promenade down past the Imperial Tarraco hotel, itself now inextricably part of the Tarragona skyline, to the amphitheatre.

The amphitheatre is first and foremost a public park. It is lunch time, and creaking swings show that children have stopped off here on their way home. There are older people, too, taking the spring sunshine, the first bougainvillaea coming into bloom, and birdsong. All manner of public spectacles took place here, including gladiators struggling with wild beasts and the occasional Christian martyrdom. Perhaps the Romans were a little ashamed of their pleasures, or the pleasures their rulers felt appropriate for the people, for the amphitheatre lies on the fringe of the Roman city. The view of the sea across the amphitheatre is unforgettable. But that can have been of little comfort to Christians being thrown to the lions.

Our own civilisation, like previous ones, has its darker side.

Completing the circuit back round to the sea end of the *rambla* – called the Balcony because of the way it dominates the railway station, the sea and the port, you can see the beginnings of the poorer quarters of the city. The tall houses are packed tightly together, their balconies festooned with potted plants and washing. At street level cars and pedestrians act out a battle for survival. Women sit out on the pavements in rickety old chairs, babies on their laps and infants under their feet. From innumerable cheap bars comes the noise of clinking glasses, juke boxes and shouted laughter, and the smell of fish and meat frying in cheap olive oil. Poverty is much the same throughout the Mediterranean. A confusion of railway sidings and cranes surround the docks and further over, on either side of the resort of Salou, are the oil terminal (which accounts for seventy-five per cent of port movements) and nuclear power station. The industrial growth of Tarragona in recent years has meant that for the first time since Roman times, Tarragona's population has exceeded 30,000, reaching 38,000 in 1950 and over 100,000 in the 1980s. This compares with a mere 5,000 in 1600 and less than that in 1700. To put the Roman figure of 30,000 in perspective, it should be remembered that until nearly 1800 the two largest towns in England outside London – Norwich and Bristol – only reached that figure. Such was imperial Tarragona.

To cater for the needs of such a large population on this relatively dry coast, large amounts of water had to be brought into the city from the rural hillsides inland. This produced one of the best loved and best preserved of all Roman monuments, the Roman aqueduct six kilometres out of town in the direction of Lleida, which brought the waters of the river Francolí into the town. Two storeys of Roman arches march across the scrubby valley to create a structure 217 metres long and 27 metres high. My children insisted on crossing it, before they were old enough to know fear, but it is not an experience I would recommend to the faint-hearted. There is no hand rail, just a low stone parapet, which separates you from the rocky valley-side below. The only sounds are the restless chirping of the crickets and the rustle of lizards as they twist away from human intruders through the scrub. Popularly, the aqueduct, like the restored Roman bridge at Martorell, where the Via Augusta crosses the river Llobregat, is known as the Devil's Bridge. It is a strange comment on the obscurantism of our medieval ancestors, that this custom of ascribing large-scale civil engineering feats to the devil should be so widespread in Europe.

There are Roman remains and reminders at Barcelona too. Barcino was firmly established by the reign of Augustus (29–14 BC) and, like Tarragona, had aqueducts to bring water into the city. It was an important place of exchange between sea and interior, and of land routes, including the one to the important settlement of Egara (modern Terrassa). Yet given its subsequent growth, little is left to see, except in the basement department of the town museum. The Roman past takes a more palpable form at Girona, ninety-five kilometres north of Barcelona, the capital of the province which stretches from the Costa Brava to the high Pyrenees and straddles the motorway to France. Here the Holy Week processions place particular emphasis upon the Roman soldiers who arrested Jesus and accompanied him to the crucifixion in the Bible story. Dressed up as Roman legionaries with their banners and eagles, they process through the narrow streets of Girona and along the Carrer de la Força, which follows exactly the old route of the Via Augusta through the city.

Yet, really to touch the magic of ancient Catalonia, there is only one place to go: Empúries, at the northern end of the Costa Brava, just fifty kilometres south of the French frontier. Some warnings are in order before you visit Empúries. Firstly, approach it from the town of L'Escala (La Escala) rather than from the pretty little stone village of Sant Martí d'Empúries as there is no longer a public entrance to the ruins on the Sant Martí side. Secondly, buy a good guidebook in a language you know – this was one place where having signs just in Catalan seemed unhelpful, and even in Catalan most were brief to the point of inscrutability. Thirdly, beware the wasps! They can take a fancy to the English traveller. The treatment, though, is brilliant; pure alcohol on the outside and strong Spanish brandy inside 'to recover from the shock' said the barman.

The barman is tall and muscular, his head a mass of curly, grey hair, his smile full of malicious good humour below a nose of impressive authority.

'You look,' I said, 'like a Roman emperor.'

'But without an empire,' came back the immediate reply.

He described himself as 'Greco-Roman', one of the eleven genuine all-the-year-round inhabitants of Sant Martí. The other thirty-nine, he explained, come up every year from Córdoba for the tourist season, and then go back home for the olive harvest.

It was here at Empúries, according to my English guidebook, that primitive Iberia had its first contact with the classical world of Greece and Rome. That, though, is an exaggeration, complicated by a confusion about the term Greeks. The Rhodians, who had established a settlement at what is now Roses, across the bay to the north of Empúries, we would recognise as Greeks. It is more difficult to see the Phocaeans as Greeks, coming as they did from the town of Phocaea in Asia Minor (modern-day Turkey). Phocaea was itself destroyed by the Persian King Cyrus in 540 BC and it was the refugees from that disaster who reinforced the settlements at Alalia (Aleria in Corsica) and another trading colony called Massalia (Marseilles). Traders from Massalia had established the *paleopolis* (old town) at Empúries in about 550 BC.

The Greeks settled by preference on islands and peninsulas, and their initial base was a small offshore island at the entrance to the Fluvià river, which with later silting up has become the rocky promontory on which Sant Martí is built. Indeed, the parish church is supposed to stand on the site of the original Greek temple, another example of those continuities of which the Mediterranean shores are so full.

In 535 BC the Carthaginians defeated the Phocaeans off Alalia in what the historian Herodotus described as the first naval battle in history, and as a result of this an earlier Phocaean settlement near present-day Málaga was also sacked. From then on, Empúries became the most important Greek settlement in Spain. As it grew, settlement extended to the mainland, where the *neapolis* or new city was established, with the port, since filled in with silt, between it and the old town on its island. This port area, now the site of fertile market gardens growing tomatoes, peppers, cucumbers, aubergines, lies inland from the narrow road that links L'Escala and Sant Martí between the sea and the ruins.

It is unfortunate in some ways that the old entrance to the site from the seashore is no longer in use. That entrance took visitors straight into the *neapolis* area between the museum and the sea. Here, you are in a Greek town and yet such is the continuity of Empúries that much of what you are looking at is actually Roman. The traders of Empúries seem to have had particular skill at staying one move ahead of political change. While the Phoenicians and Carthaginians reinforced their bases in southern Spain, the Phocaeans at Massalia and Empúries allied themselves with the emerging power in the Mediterranean – Rome. A Roman expeditionary force, landed at Empúries in 218 BC and subsequently established headquarters at Tarraco. The Iberian tribes initially opposed Roman rule, but were overpowered by Cato following a second landing at Empúries in 195 BC.

It is all too easy to let the atmosphere of the place overtake you with its strong emotional appeal. The sun beats down, and a characteristic Empúries sight is a knot of visitors gathered under a shady pine – the cypresses may look authentic, but it is the pines that are the natives of this coast and give the better shade as well as their warm fragrance. And the blue Mediterranean sparkles between cypresses and pines and classical columns and the bulk of the Greek and Roman breakwaters linking the outlying rocks along a stretch of beach nearly the whole way from L'Escala to Empúries: protection from the sea but also openness to the sea the whole way from L'Escala to the Punta Falconera, where the Pyrenees meet the sea beyond Roses. It was these breakwaters that also gave access to the interior and the rich agricultural lands of the Empordà. Here, then, is the proper setting for things Roman – not Bath or St Albans in cold, wet, southern England but Tarragona and Empúries on the edge of the great tideless sea.

After midday an onshore breeze sets in, and there is much else to see at Empúries. In the museum are classical statues with faces distant in time yet close in space to the broad foreheads, wide eyes, hooked noses and small mouths of the Catalan people on the beach. It is rich in pottery, which helps to establish a continuity with the traditional Catalan pottery manufactured not so many miles away at La Bisbal. The finest of the Greek and Roman pottery makes it clear that Catalan pottery is a peasant, or popular, descendant of classical wares. Yet in its simplicity and solidity it also has its own roots and values in the material culture of the people of the red lands of the Empordà, who were there before the Phocaeans and were still there, albeit modified in race and culture and language, when the Romans were long gone.

In the Roman part of the town on the hilltop there is an extensive religious area which contained a series of temples to the various Roman gods, their ground-plans little different from those of primitive Romanesque churches of a millennium later. Excavation and restoration is continuing in this part of the Roman town. Another element of continuity is the forum, the place of

public discussion of public affairs. The forum is a direct anteced-
ent of the *plaça* of medieval Catalan towns, even to the custom of
arcading the streets which led into it. Likewise, the porticoed
atrium of the larger Roman villas is a forerunner of the traditional
Spanish house with its central patio. The Roman town has a
spaciousness not found in the crowded streets of the neapolis,
and again this contrast of busy crowded alleyways and expansive
avenues and squares is a contrast not uncommon in modern
Catalonia. The pedestrian precinct, a recent innovation in towns
such as Barcelona, Girona and Lleida, was pioneered in the
Roman forum at Empúries.

The sun starts to set early at Empúries and there are soon a
few empty patches of shade on the beaches. The light is ethereal
and majestic, the sea darkening to deepest ultramarine towards
the horizon, shading to oranges and greens in the shallow,
sandy waters by the shoreline, the sand itself the lightest of
fawns. At its back, the dark green of pines and a sky beginning
to turn pink on its western fringes. To drive slowly back across
the Empordà in this evening light is to share a moment of
peaceful serenity. The maize, mimosas, poplars as green as
green, the Ter river as richly muddied as Louisiana, the cosiness
and security of this rich and ancient land. No wonder one of
the most haunting songs of the folk singer Lluís Llach translates
roughly as 'Bury me out in the Empordà'! It is strange as strange
to reflect at this point in the silky, golden evening that from
1970 to 1974, Llach was banned from singing in Spain because
his music was thought to be too political . . . increasingly those
Franco years seem like a bizarre interruption of the tranquil
course of Catalan history.

But this, of course, is the fantastic rubbish that only such an
evening could produce. Turbulence and violent change have
been the iron laws of this land. Empúries itself never fully
recovered from the barbarian invasions of the third century AD,
and unlike Barcino and Tarraco was never completely rebuilt.
The city continued to house a bishopric through the Visigothic
period of Spanish history between the eventual fall of the Roman
Empire and the Arab invasions, although a seventh-century
Norman invasion had probably swept away what little remained
of the city well before the Arabs invaded in or about AD 718.
Feudal warring among the early Christian counties established
by Charlemagne south of the Pyrenees as a bulwark against

further Arab expansion into Europe, the silting up of the river, and the generally unhealthy, marshy nature of the site, all contributed to the decision of the Count of Empúries to rebuild his capital in the tenth century at Castelló d'Empúries, some miles inland. The ruins of Empúries gradually sank beneath the sands, driven by the *Tramuntana* winds that are so fierce on this part of the coast. But the memory of a once great city never died.

What, then, does it all mean to the Catalans themselves and to the peoples of northern Europe, who crowd the shores in these parts every summer? People go on holiday either to confirm their culture or to deny it. Blackpool and Katmandu represent two ideal types of holiday. Blackpool represents to the working class a positive image of their lives and values. Similarly with festival-going, to Bath or Aldeburgh for classical music, to Edinburgh or Brighton for dance and theatre. Such holidays encapsulate a positive view of the holiday-makers which carries them through the rest of the year. On the other hand, travellers to Katmandu, or to the high Andes or to Outer Mongolia, go there precisely because of a sense of dissatisfaction and unfulfilment in their everyday lives. The holiday here may be full of material hardships but offers a positive experience which sustains life as much as the other sort, but this time by confirming for people that they can be 'other', that their everyday lives do not exhaust the possibilities of being human.

The coast of Catalonia belongs to the first group. For northern Europeans, with their emphasis on physical fitness and athletic prowess, the Mediterranean allows a direct expression of the physical side of life in a way in which the cold, damp climates of northwestern Europe do not. For them nudity and near nudity are not just added extras to Mediterranean holidays, but an integral part of the experience. And it is an experience that the Catalans have embraced enthusiastically. Tourism brings prosperity to people who earn a living from it, but for other Catalans it is an extension of the public, open-air life of their cities, towns and villages.

The lunch-time and evening promenades are an opportunity to see and be seen, to show off or just to gossip and feel part of a more exciting life than the family circle or the television can provide. Just as Catalans prefer a crowded bar or restaurant to an empty one, they revel in the noise and sociability of the beach. They bring picnics, which often constitute substantial meals, and tables, chairs and bright umbrellas to provide an island of shade on the burning sand. The whole family comes, and although grandparents may pretend to be shocked by the endless parade of tanned, lithe bodies, it is hard to escape the impression that they enjoy the beach life as much as the younger members of the family.

Despite the prohibitions of the Franco years, when English girls were regularly in trouble with the Spanish police for wearing bikinis on the beach, Catholic Spain has always had a popular tolerance of the body and of sex which contradicted official attitudes. In the 1960s, I remember travelling across the heart of Spain from Madrid to Córdoba in summer, and noticing the shoals of naked children bathing in the rivers, and women sitting outside their houses in dusty little villages breast-feeding their babies and chatting to neighbours without embarrassment. The informality of Catalan beaches today is not just something that the Swedes, French and Germans have brought with them.

In artistic terms, the cult of the physical is best expressed in the movement known as *Noucentisme* (the 1900s), which on the one hand makes claim to being an experience of modernity, but also looks directly back to the Mediterranean past. This group of painters established an image of the Mediterranean world which both reflected the material world they lived in but, and in turn, has conditioned our minds as we look back from image to reality, from the picture to the sea, the vineyards, the olive groves and the pine trees of the Catalan coast. One of the influences was certainly the excavations at Empúries and the art objects of ancient Greece and Rome being uncovered there, but although classicism was an important influence on these painters, they attempted to express in their work the Mediterranean spirit rather than the academic details of classical art. One of the key figures in this movement was not a Catalan at all, but a Uruguayan, Joaquín Torres-García, who lived and worked in Barcelona until 1920. A typical work of his is *Orange-trees facing the sea* (1920) in Barcelona's modern art museum. The Mediterranean sea is always the backdrop to these pictures, the middle-ground is the Catalan landscape, and the foreground contains emblematic figures, in this case two lightly clad women and a basket of oranges, as in a still life. Torres-García used classical myths and legends in the murals that he executed using fresco technique in public buildings in Barcelona in the second decade of the century.

Those in the Saló de Sant Jordi (St George's Hall) in the Generalitat can still be seen and make a striking contrast with the Gothic informality of the orange-tree patio onto which the Hall opens.

The Sitges artist Joaquim Sunyer shows the influence of another great Mediterranean painter, Cézanne. Cézanne had reintroduced to painting the great classical theme of nudes in landscape, and this theme of figures, clothed or unclothed, in a natural setting, is taken up by Sunyer in paintings such as *Cala Forn* (1917), again in the Barcelona modern art museum. There is a distant view of sea and coast, but the main interest is in the foreground figures (here clothed in simple, loose-fitting garments) and their elemental still-life possessions – a *porró* (a long-spouted drinking vessel which can be passed from person to person), a water melon, peaches, a water bottle. Where Torres-García appealed directly to classical stories in his murals, Sunyer created a new secular mythology which fitted in well with the mood of resurgent nationalism in Catalonia in the 1910s. The sculptures by Clarà, one of which is in the Casals garden at Sant Salvador, were another essential part of this movement, with the female nude as the major theme. In an astonishing coincidence, another Catalan sculptor, but this time from French Catalonia, Aristide Maillol, was developing along similar lines and quite independently. His nude called *La Méditerranée*, in the gardens of the Louvre in Paris, dates from 1902 to 1905, before the first stirrings of *Noucentisme*, and it was some years before contact was established.

After 1917 it is hard to write of *Noucentisme* as a movement with any kind of coherent philosophy. However, the style of *Noucentisme* influenced Josep Obiols, who continued to work in a recognisably *noucentista* style during the 1920s and 1930s, and in a wide variety of formats: paintings, book covers and illustrations, posters, stamps, frescoes, concert programmes. The sum total of his work represents many of the most humane aspects of Catalan life in the years immediately before the Civil War. He was a 'public artist', an artist at the service of his nation. This is embodied in one of his best-loved images – the 1921 poster for A.P.E.C. (L'Associació Protectora de l'Ensenyança Catalana – Catalan Educational Association), showing a child striding through an idyllic, stylised landscape of birds and flowers. The poster he made for the first congress of the A.P.E.C. in 1936 shows a more serious-faced child against a more urban setting, a

35

flat-roofed, very modern looking public building. Obiols was caught up in both the Civil War, during which he designed paper money and stamps for the Generalitat, and the repression that followed, when he retreated to painting mostly portraits of friends and family. His public work from the post-war period consists largely of murals at the monastery of Montserrat, which kept the torch of Catalan culture alight during the dark years of the Franco dictatorship.

Obiols is above all the artist of children. They speak of both timelessness and tradition, but also of the urgency of the moment. A task of a humane society is to love and care for its children, and that was an integral part of Obiols' vision. A large exhibition of his work was held in the Palau de la Virreina in the *rambla* in Barcelona in 1990. This is the chief exhibition space of the Ajuntament (town council) and their policy of free admission for senior citizens gave a particular atmosphere to this show. It was clear from the enthusiastic response of these older people, and listening to snatches of conversation as I went round, that many of these people were recognising images they remembered from books they had read at school and posters they had seen on the streets. A nation needs its Obiols as well as its Picasso.

I have tried to identify in an artistic movement those images which appealed to the Catalans themselves but which also, fifty years later, were to provide an essential image of the country in the development of modern tourism. Through *Noucentisme*, the Catalans identified themselves with the history and values of the Mediterranean, a rich landscape in which the human drama was played out against the timeless backcloth of the smooth blue sea. There is, of course, a negative side to all this. Tourism has spoilt so much of the Catalan coast by the over-development of towns and villages, the uncontrolled speculative building of hotels, villas and apartment blocks, and the curiously named 'urbanisations', the housing estates that spoilt the countryside without any of the civilising virtues of the truly urban.

Much of what I have recounted in this chapter may seem far removed from everyday life in Catalonia. So I want to end far from the Mediterranean itself, far from golden Tarragona or silver Empúries, in the little town of Balaguer, north of Lleida, on the road to the distant Pyrenees and to return, finally, to the town square or *plaça*.

Balaguer was once the capital of the Urgell, the county that extended south from the Pyrenees and marked the southern extension of Catalonia during the centuries of conflict between Christians and Muslims. There are fine houses along the river front facing blocks of modern flats set in grassland on the opposite bank. But the heart of the town is a large, arcaded square sloping gently from north to south. Here, in the shade of the thirty-eight plane trees which mark out the public space, the people of Balaguer walk and talk or sit and rest, taking the sun in winter and enjoying the shade in summer. The sandy-coloured mass of the church on the hill rises above the roofs, its clock tower clearly visible, and next to it are the remains of a vast medieval castle. A solitary traffic policeman, one of life's natural depressives, keeps a tight hold on would-be parking offenders with his shrill whistle and admonishing index finger.

The red and green umbrellas of the café on the top side of the square extend across the roadway beneath the plane trees. People come and go, pause and linger, some to sit for hours eating, drinking, reading the newspapers, talking of this or that which seems so important today but will be forgotten tomorrow. They lean towards one another as they talk, an important point emphasised by a hand gripping an elbow, disagreement marked by a wagging finger that echoes the policeman's. Interminable handshakes and kisses on both cheeks are exchanged as friends and family arrive and depart. It is a scene which is repeated time and time again in Catalonia, but here with a style that speaks in clear terms of a public, open space. The *plaça* at Balaguer symbolises for me a vital element of continuity in the Mediterranean world, extending far beyond the immediate proximity of the sea. It is a space to be in, rather than merely to pass through. A direct descendant of the Roman forum. A social work of art.

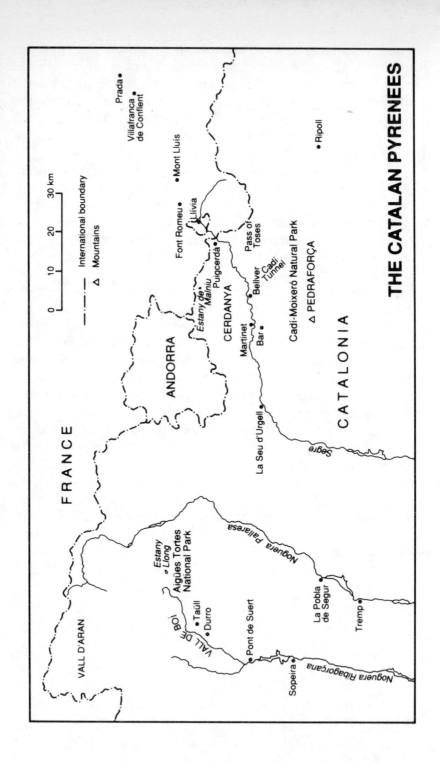

THE CATALAN PYRENEES

Chapter 4

Romanesque Mountains

In general, the English used by the various Catalan tourist bodies has improved markedly over recent years. Gone are the days when John Langdon-Davies (in his 1953 book *Gatherings from Catalonia*) could get a rise out of the 'unspeakable white houses' at Cadaqués, or of the solemn pronouncement that Barcelona streets are lined by banana trees (the Catalan word means both banana and plane tree). However, there are numerous references in tourist literature to Catalonia, a 'millennial country'. The phrase is unfortunate in English, with its suggestion of 'the end is nigh'. But the meaning is clear. One of the points the Generalitat has tried to emphasise in the ten years of its existence is the sense of historical identity of Catalonia as a nation.

In a long conversation with me in April 1990, Josep Maria Ainaud de Lasarte, a Barcelona town councillor for the CiU (Conservative Nationalist Party) emphasised the importance of two things – Christianity and democracy. At first sight he is the archetypal conservative politician, a silver-haired elder statesman sitting comfortably at his desk in a book-lined office on the seventh floor of a Barcelona office block. But towards the end of our talk he told me a little about his activities during the Franco years. He had been a friend of Casals, 'although we didn't share the same political views', and his special job had been ferrying people across the Pyrenees who had their own very good reasons for not wanting to pass an official checkpoint.

He claimed that the Muslim influence in Catalonia had been insignificant and that Judaism had always been confined to the ghetto. He saw the notion of democratic participation as important both to the development of political institutions such as the *corts* (parliament), the Consell de Cent (Barcelona town council) and to economic development through markets, guilds and the

Consulat de Mar (Maritime Law Tribunal). One-man rule he rejected as 'oriental'.

The period after the collapse of the Roman Empire in Spain, from about AD 400, though clearly a time of turbulence and upheaval, was not a 'dark age' as it was in England, where the Latin language and Christian religion disappeared completely and a long period of anarchy ensued. The language – the forms of vulgar Latin spoken by the ordinary people of the Iberian peninsula – the Christian religion, Roman law and urban ideas were taken on by the Visigoths, who, by the time they reached Spain, had had their own culture transmogrified by the contact with Rome. They were Christians of sorts, though they remained Arians until AD 589.

My own understanding of this period in Catalan history was changed dramatically many years ago when I first visited Terrassa, an important textile town in the Vallès region inland from Barcelona, to which it is joined by a narrow-gauge railway originating in the heart of Barcelona – the Plaça de Catalunya. Narrow-gauge, of course, is a relative notion. It is narrow-gauge by Spanish standards, but is in fact the normal UK gauge.

In the unlikely setting of this industrial town is one of the most remarkable groups of churches anywhere in Europe – the parish church, Sant Pere, the cathedral church of Santa Maria and the baptistery of Sant Miquel. Terrassa has been mentioned once before, as the Roman city of Egara, and it is this site which the three churches occupy. It became a bishopric in AD 450 and remained one until the Arab invasions some 250 years later. The restoration and the documentation of these three churches was largely the work at the end of the nineteenth century of the historian, architect and nationalist politician Josep Puig i Cadalfach, a name that will recur in this book.

It is the baptistery that most perfectly conserves the feel of this early stage of Christianity. It is hard to put a date on these buildings, but the baptistery is essentially a sixth- or seventh-century building, a Greek cross with tiny chapels at each angle and an apse at the east side which is horse-shoe-shaped inside and polygonal outside. The whole site forms roughly a square. At the centre of the church is a cupola held up by eight ancient pillars, the shafts and Corinthian capitals of which have in turn been reassembled from earlier structures. Below this cupola is a reconstruction of the pool where these early Christians were baptised. The importance of baptism in this heroic period of Christianity, when it was spreading to become the dominant religion of western Europe, is clearly stated. And the whole womb-like closeness of the church emphasises this sense of rebirth, the need of people to feel safe – and saved – which is as ancient as humankind and which is clearly a strong psychological impulse in the success of Christianity.

Santa Maria, the cathedral church of the Visigoths, is more like an historical puzzle. The mosaic paving outside is probably from the first Christian church on the site. The rectangular apse of this early church and sepulchral crypts have been identified from excavations beneath the later nave. For English visitors, there is particular interest in the twelfth-century Romanesque paintings in a transept apse of St Thomas-à-Becket, found beneath later Gothic murals, demonstrating how quickly the cult of this unfortunate English saint spread through Europe. Sant Pere, the parish church, is clearly Visigothic at the east end, with a three-lobed apse, but the nave of the church is twelfth-century Romanesque in the Lombard style, like so many other Catalan churches.

The invasion of the Arabs at the beginning of the eighth century was a decisive event, exposing the internal feuding and weaknesses of the Visigothic kingdom. The relaunching of Christian Spain towards the end of that century involved tighter organisation in smaller units. In 785 the people of Girona, followed by those of the Urgell and the Cerdanya, acknowledged allegiance to Ludovico Pio, son of Charlemagne. This led to the reconquest of Barcelona in 801 and the setting up of a number of counties on the Spanish side of the Pyrenees with independent political, military and judicial control. At the same time, the church established a network of parishes in the newly reconquered areas. Prominent among these counties were Urgell, the Cerdanya, Berga, Empúries, Besalú. In the next two centuries, two processes were at work. Firstly, the beginnings of the ascendancy of the Count of Barcelona. Under Guifré (Wilfred) the Hairy, the counties of Osona, Girona and Barcelona were effectively joined together, and the influence of Barcelona acknowledged as far away as the Conflent, beyond the Pyrenees. Secondly, in the years following the death of Guifré the Hairy in 897, the counties south of the Pyrenees gradually asserted their independence of their Frankish overlords. Thus, following the Arab raid on Barcelona in 965, Count Borell II refused to serve the Franks in a counter-raid. But neither of these processes should be overestimated. Contact with post-Carolingian Europe remained strong, and the independent power of the isolated Pyrenean counties lasted well into the eleventh and twelfth centuries.

It was indeed this contact with the wider world of Europe that opened one of the great periods of Catalan art – the Romanesque – from about the year AD 1000. An essential feature of Romanesque is that it is a European movement which spread with great speed across the continent. The Romanesque existed as a civil style used in castles, houses and bridges. However, the impulse behind its spread was the religious reform of the Benedictines, radiating out from the Abbey of Cluny in France. The paintings and carvings in their religious buildings illustrated Bible stories and the contrasting fates of the chosen and the damned, providing an effective way of bringing enlightenment to the people. The Benedictines set a standard which was copied in churches great and small throughout Catalonia, but especially in the churches of the Pyrenean valleys. Massive masonry was used to support barrel vaults; systems of decoration, especially the blind arcades of the Lombard bands, were introduced by travelling bands of Italian masons, who spread this particular influence through Provence to the Catalan counties.

The settings of the buildings themselves are the most striking feature about the Pyrenean churches. Most of their splendid wall paintings, altarpieces and crosses were removed long ago to the safe keeping of the Museu d'Art de Catalunya in Barcelona's National Palace on Montjuïc, a javelin-throw from the Olympic stadium. Cela is especially bitter about the removal of these treasures from the Pyrenees to Barcelona. He complains that the money spent on looking after them and paying the employees of the museum would be better spent repairing leaky roofs and restoring the original homes of these works of art. He sees Catalonia sharing in the Spanish problem of over-centralisation, with Barcelona feeding off the fruits of the Catalan provinces just as the Catalans complain that Madrid feeds off Barcelona.

It is a long way from Barcelona to the Vall de Boí in the Pyrenees. My own journey began on a rainy morning in August along the perpetual roadworks of the A7 from Martorell up to the tunnel at El Bruch. Gradually the clouds lifted off the mountains of Montserrat, and that magical jagged profile appeared. But the sun did not appear until I reached the dry lands around Cervera, already in Lleida province, with their few villages dominated by the characteristic combination of church and castle. There is a dramatic change as soon as you cross the Urgell canal, for here the irrigated lands of Lleida begin, with head-high maize alternating with fields of ripe peaches, apples and pears as far as the eye can see. North from Balaguer, you must make a lengthy diversion into Aragon, though without necessarily leaving Catalan-speaking areas. For Catalan is spoken along a strip stretching twenty kilometres west of the Noguera Ribagorçana including the cheerful little town of Bena-varri (Benarrabe) with its bustling cafés and restaurants. Eventu-ally the road turns back east to join the river, the offical frontier between Catalonia and Aragon. It is now late afternoon and the Pyrenees seem to be closing in all around us, with already deep shade on the west side of the valley. Above Pont de Suert, there is a signpost to the right indicating the rather cramped entrance to the Vall de Boí.

The Vall de Boí is another of Catalonia's well-kept secrets, and even in midsummer its camp sites, hotels and national park seem almost exclusively populated by Catalans, plus some Valencians, who are Catalan-speaking in any case. First impressions are of rushing water, pine and oak woods and high pastures with limestone outcrops. It is an intimate countryside, at least until you get to the 2,000-metre contour in the national park. Where we have pitched our tent, over the hedge as full of brambles and old man's beard as any in England, is a field with a haystack, that curious and very ancient haystack with the pole in the middle and the hay apparently carelessly tossed up against it to make a conical mound, part of our common European heritage. The trees in the valley are lime, ash, pine, hazel and walnut. There are midges here, but the few mosquitoes seem indolent and droopy. Perhaps the air is too thin and cold for them, with a northwest wind setting in after the day's cold front has passed. Certainly, I have experienced few starry nights as brilliant as that first night in the shelter of the Vall de Boí, sparkling in their infinite and untouchable beauty in the clear mountain air – the Plough, Orion, Mars, the Milky Way. In universal terms, it is but a few moments that separate us from the people who created, here in the Vall de Boí, a series of masterpieces of Christian art. And in some strange, mysterious way those intensely religious artists are a bridge between the purposeful doing of human society and the purposeless being of infinite space.

In the morning, the sky is purest china-blue. The sun appears late over the thickly wooded hillside, a giant, glittering star. Each leaf on each tree in our meadow is a rich pattern of light and shade.

Our first church up the valley is Coll, set apart from its little village amid walnut trees. The blind arcading here is not just around the apse, but continues along the nave and gabled west end as well. There is dressed stone inside and out, including some pretty, pink granite. We are shown round by a knowledgeable old woman who is the self-appointed custodian of the church. She shows us the 400-year-old priest seats:

'Made of walnut.'

'Of course! We saw them growing down the lane.'

'Now please wait. I must greet my next visitors.'

She makes a lively living from her modern pilgrims. The roof is slate and the tower, one hundred years later than the body of the church, is square and squat and simple with a little slate cap that appears on all the towers in the valley. Anywhere else it would be remarkable. Here, this church is the norm. The administrative district of Barruera, named after its most populated village, has no less than fifteen Romanesque churches built in the eleventh and twelfth centuries, most of which have apses, slim square towers surmounted by slate caps and carved porches.

In the Generalitat's excellent guide to the architectural heritage of Catalonia, available in English, Santa Maria de Coll does not even merit an entry. To see why, it is necessary to go a few miles further up the valley, to the church of Santa Eulàlia de Erill-La-Vall. This is a single nave with semicircular apse and side-apse chapels. But it is the tower that imposes itself on the visitor, slim and elegant with five stages of paired Lombardy arches, blind arcades and cog-work decoration. On the south side of the nave there is interesting stonework with rows of thin slate between semi-dressed granite blocks. But the north side facing the Pyrenean houses with their pretty wooden balconies is even more distinctive. Across a flower-strewn graveyard is an open porch stretching the full length of the nave and supported by three elegant round stone columns, for all the world like an Italian Renaissance loggia. There is one other in the valley, at Durro, which is in the process of restoration. These porch arcades

44

provided some protection against the harsh climate of this high valley and were used for village meetings of one sort or another. They are rather unusual in Catalonia but much more common in the Castilian provinces of Ávila and Segovia, where they can be much more clearly identified with the rights and privileges given to the townspeople by the king. In Castile the Romanesque style emerged during a relatively pacific period, whereas here in Catalonia it coincided with the period at the beginning of the eleventh century when Arab raids into the Christian counties were a constant threat and defence a prime consideration in church-building.

If Erill-La-Vall is emotionally the most satisfying of the churches in the valley, it is the two churches at Taüll which are the best known and, in some ways, most bizarre. Here, everything is subjugated to the tower and I have often wondered exactly what lies behind the existence of two churches in this small village: Sant Climent consecrated on 11 December 1123 and Santa Maria consecrated the day after, 12 December 1123. At Sant Climent you can climb the tower if you have the stomach for it. The blind arcades are extremely simple and the paired arches occupy much of each of the six stages, giving a sense of openness and lightness to this slim tower. To put it another way, you feel constantly in danger of falling out of the tower onto the Romanesque art industry below – the cafés, restaurants, camp site and apartment houses. The bells are still in place, and the largest is exquisitely carved with scenes from the life of the Virgin. If Sant Climent seems given over to the tourist industry, Santa Maria, in the centre of the village, is still the church in use, with its more restrained, four-stage bell tower firmly locked. Outside, a wooden bar, set up for a party the previous month, is still in position between two of the apses, with empty bottles and used plastic cups still strewn beneath it. I wondered idly if Taüll might secretly be a hotbed of paganism, and if this might explain why it needed two such grand churches.

Missing from inside Santa Eulàlia de Erill-La-Vall is a twelfth-century sculptural group of the Descent from the Cross, part of which is in the collection of the Museu Episcopal (Bishop's Museum) in Vic and the other part at Montjuïc. A sixteenth-century altarpiece has gone a different direction to the Diocesan Museum at La Seu d'Urgell. At Taüll there are reproductions to replace the missing murals. However, they are very much second best. At Sant Climent, the artificial lighting emphasises the thinness of the colours, while at Santa Maria the great apse mural of the Three Kings only achieves its impact because of the delicate golden evening light coming through the west window and illuminating the nave up to the apse. This image fills the curved vault of the apse while below are full-length figures of the gospel writers and below that again round medallions of mythical animals whose ancestry can be traced right back to ancient Egypt. The exhibition at the Museu d'Art de Catalunya has attempted to re-create the setting of the original church, but of course what can never be re-created in the heart of the city are the rocky limestone bluffs and green alpine meadows of the Pyrenees, the distant sound of a cow- or sheep-bell through the still, clear air. The great image of the apse at Sant Climent is the pancreator, Christ as omnipotent god, creator, law giver and saviour of the world, surrounded by angels, the great mystery of God become human, of the union of the spiritual and the physical. It is a compelling image, but not quite perfect. At Barcelona you see the image itself, but without the setting, at Taüll the setting with a mere copy of the image.

At another turn of the valley lies Durro, where the Generalitat is supposed to be working on the restoration of the church of Santa Maria. Its porch arcade is even grander than that of Erill-La-Vall, with blind arcades and decorative band-work in the stone. Here the square tower is fortress-like in its imposing height and massive cross-section, and I find both this tower and that at Sant Joan de Boí more satisfying than the nervous heights of Sant Climent de Taüll. There are flights of swallows cavorting around it, and a distant view of the hermitage of Sant Quirze amid the meadows and the mountains rising bare and almost white into the cloudless blue sky. It is a cheerful village in which holiday-makers and farmers mix happily in the local bar and the cottage gardens are full of hollyhocks and tomatoes and apple trees. It is Sunday, but still a working day in the valley. The track up to the hermitage is completely blocked by a truck outside a house where the vegetable garden has runner beans and marrows:

'Who does the truck belong to?'

'A stranger. He's come to buy stock.'

'And you've no idea where he is?'

'Somewhere up behind. I'll go and have a look.'

This conversation is repeated several times with different passers-by. A few minues later the stranger returns, large and bearded, in corduroy trousers and check shirt, his face weather-beaten from constant exposure to the rigours of mountain life. He comes bearing a sheep, a living icon of the Good Shepherd from a long-forgotten wall painting.

The hermitage, when we bump to a halt outside it, is a tiny nave and single apse church with magnificent views and again the distant tolling of animal bells on the high meadows, so far away that we are unable to make them out with any certainty. In these silent high places any sound carries with absolute clarity. But we are not alone. The Catalan custom of picnicking in high remote places, preferably with company, is at work here. Its deepest roots probably lie in the communal pilgrimages from town or village to a nearby hilltop shrine. They became opportunities for eating and drinking, music and dancing. In more recent years such outings have become part of the urban tradition of heading off to the mountains in search of the 'authentically Catalan', with family and friends, or as part of an organised group of scouts or guides, or one of the many *excursionista* clubs which exist in Catalonia. There are several large family groups and a mother and daughter. A fire is alight to cook meat on, and a naked child is lifted up to sample the icy cold crystalline delights of the fountain. Three teenage boys with a simple electronic keyboard provide their contemporary version of Pan's pipes as we eat our bread and cheese and fruit leaning against the wall of the hermitage. The first afternoon breeze stirs in the ash trees, a lizard slips quickly from a hole in the church wall, straight across the newspaper I am reading and into the bushes. A car bomb in Burgos, a crisis in the Arabian Gulf, traffic accidents, cocaine . . . A few swallows begin their evening hunt for food. Three harmless clouds, uncertain whether to be balls of cotton wool or fleecy lambs, sail harmlessly along on the breeze. If places have a spirit that looks after them, then Sant Quirze de Durro will live for ever.

It is only as a footnote to this Pyrenean picnic that I mention the fact that this tiny chapel is represented in the Barcelona museum by a delightful painted wooden altar-front, completed in about 1100, of the martyrdom of Santa Julita and her three-year-old son, Quirze. There is no understatement here, and the episodes of violent death and torture are as gruesomely portrayed as any of the battle scenes from the Bayeux tapestry. Harold may have been killed by an arrow in his eye, but at least he didn't get nails hammered into his eyes, sawn in half or end up with his baby in a cooking pot. It is difficult to see what solace the local people found from the hardship of life in these sternly moralistic pictures. They portray the evil of humankind as surely as the great murals of Taüll portray the goodness identified with the story of Christ.

If the churches of the Vall de Boí give some indication of how Romanesque art developed in Catalonia, its roots are best seen in the great Benedictine abbeys of Ripoll, which dates from 880, and Sant Pere de Rodes, established in 934. The Benedictines brought order to the conduct of the religious life, but were also capable and enterprising businessmen who made their monasteries centres of material wealth and power. Ripoll is a town I have known for many years, situated as it is on one of my favourite railway lines. It is another of those lines which begins in the heart of Barcelona, at the underground Plaça de Catalunya station. Circumventing the green hills of Montseny, it crosses the plain of Vic and eventually plunges through a deep tunnel to reach the Cerdanya and the French frontier at Puigcerdà. Ripoll grew up around its monastery, founded by Guifré the Hairy, a substantial town with iron and textile industries, but too far away from the heart of Catalan industry for its industrial strength ever to overpower the counterweight of the medieval monastery. It has survived much – an earthquake, fire and pillage by the nineteenth-century anticlerical liberals, and the all too complete attentions of its restorer, Elias Rogent, this latter trial taking place between 1886 and 1893. It is the mid-twelfth-century porch at Ripoll that takes away any doubts the visitor may have. It is more a triumphal arch than a church doorway, extending the full width of the nave. Taken together, the scenes are a vivid dictionary of the stories and scenes that proliferate in Romanesque art – the saints, especially the near life-size figures of Saints Peter and Paul that flank the doorway, Bible scenes, especially the vision of the Apocalypse, saints, angels and Christ in Majesty. There are also carvings of the signs of the Zodiac, real and fantastic animals, scenes of daily life taken from the calendar of the seasons – ploughing, hunting, sowing and reaping – and scenes of warfare.

Saint Pere de Rodes is a monastery capping the extension of the Pyrenees, which stick out into the sea just south of the French border and which end in the great cliffs and lighthouse of Cap de Creus. But for years I shared with Rose Macaulay a failure actually to visit it. 'The shadow of this mighty ruin haunted me, and haunts me still,' she wrote in *Fabled Shore*. I had identified it in my mind with those symbols of unattainable spirituality she was so fond of.

In July 1990, I was joined on a visit to Sant Pere by a young, bespectacled Pole, Jurek Afanasjew, who was making a film for Polish television about Catalonia. Jurek spoke neither Catalan nor Castilian but he knew in Polish the Lluís Llach song of the transition to democracy in Catalonia and Spain, with its triumphant chorus:

> Si jo l'estiro fort per aquí
> i tu l'estires fort per allà,
> segur que tomba, tomba, tomba,
> i ens podrem alliberar.

(If I pull it hard this way / and you pull it hard that way, / it's bound to turn / and we shall be free.)

Our assault began on the land side of Sant Pere, at the village of Vilajuïga, a simple little village minding its own business in the summer sunshine. A woman was organising a clothes stall from the back of a Renault 4 van outside the simple church with its open stone belfry.

We had a long climb. First of all the fields and orchards of the Empordà give way to a typical Mediterranean landscape of olives and vines. But higher up this, too, gives way to the coarse, sweet-smelling scrub of the maquis, then to equally sweet-smelling pine woods and eventually to bare rock. Jurek is filming out of the open car window and the deep growl of an overworked engine is the bass to the soprano chirping of the crickets singing at the tops of their merry voices. Below, the railway disappears into its tunnel heading for the coast and France, the N11 road winds across the lowest part of the ridge that joins us to the Pyrenees. Driving cannot have been so different in the days when Rose Macaulay complained of the potholes and the punctures which were the inevitable accompaniments to a car trip through Spain.

Then suddenly the sea, the coast disappearing in the mist

towards France, and Port de la Selva beneath us with its outriders of marinas, camp sites and villas. And the sea mist rolling in grey-blue swathes across the hills from the direction of Cap de Creus. The sea where the pirates roamed. Sometimes the pirates came ashore and did what pirates were good at: raping, pillaging and looting. Occasionally a rich man or an official was taken prisoner in the hope of a ransom. Fit young men would be taken for slave labour in the galleys, and young women would be traded in the markets of North Africa. When the threat of piracy began to evaporate, especially after the defeat of the Turkish navies by Don Juan of Austria at the battle of Lepanto in 1571, the people moved back down to the coast, abandoning hilly rural settlements like Santa Creu de Rodes with its ruined pre-Romanesque church of Santa Elena.

Sant Pere avoided the fate of other Catalan monasteries, destroyed by liberal anticlericalism in the nineteenth century, because by 1800 it had been completely abandoned. But the decline of Sant Pere began a long time before this, its rise and fall matching the rise and fall of feudalism and monasticism. A priory in the ninth century, the great church was consecrated in 1022, and around it flourished the buildings of a monastic order devoted to the word of God, but also to the ownership of land and the production of wine and oil, those staples of the Mediterranean economy.

What the visitor sees at Sant Pere is the patient work of twentieth-century archaeology and restoration. Yet it preserves something of the Romantic ruins that Rose Macaulay surmised nearly half a century ago, with birds flitting around between the massive square columns and Corinthian capitals of the church, from which spring both the nave and aisle arches. The treasures of Sant Pere were scattered across the Western world, old and new, and there is little to distract one from the heroic poetry of pink, grey and creamy stone against a dark blue sky, with alpine plants growing over ruined arches and doorways. Current restoration work is being funded by the European Community and there is an excellent historical commentary in seven languages, which you can listen to gazing at the church and the coast and sea. But the most impressive and most characteristic images of Sant Pere are its towers, the austere slim fortress tower and the church tower which achieves power by its sheer size, but lightness, too, by the frequent piercings of different shapes and sizes.

An additional climb is recommended up the tangled path through maquis and briars to the castle on the 670-metre-high hilltop. There is sufficient of the ruin standing to provide a little shade, and a riot of wild flowers – pinks, thistles, succulents – and of insects – dragonflies, bluebottles, fritillary butterflies – to delight the eye. Over it swoops a solitary swallow. The view is immense. The view that made it a perfect watchtower for pirates. To the south the coast towards Empúries, the plain of the Empordà, green and ochre, traced by roads and speckled with villages. To the east the roads snake down towards Port de la Selva, with its glittering sands in front of modest houses that have resisted the appeal of the high-rise apartment blocks. To the north sparkling little Llança and the tiny coves up beyond Portbou and into France. To the west, the sierra, first falling away to the low ridge where the main road crosses it and then rising again to the misty Pyrenees. Little wonder with these bountiful lands at their feet that the Benedictines of Sant Pere de Rodes fell victim to the joys of material wealth. Or that the peasants came to hate them for it.

Chapter 5

Arabs, Christians and Jews

In the cathedral museum at Girona is one of medieval Catalonia's most delightful and accessible works of art – the tapestry of the Creation. It is unique, or at least I do not know of any equivalent work of art, a colourful piece of embroidery dating from the eleventh or twelfth century. It is about nothing more nor less than creation itself, the created world as it appeared to medieval Catalans, with the sun and stars, the winds, the months, days and seasons, the plants and animals and fishes. The centre of it is the figure of a rather friendly, humble-looking God, looking almost embarrassed about the variety of nature he has created. The words, 'And God said "Let there be light", and there was light' are embroidered around him. A great circle is divided like cake slices with the upper ones representing the inhabitants of heaven, and the lower ones the created earth, Eve emerging from the side of a naked, puzzled Adam, the fishes of the sea, the birds of the air, and the animals on dry land sporting around another figure of Adam. The circle then becomes a square with the four winds, 'green men', sitting on gigantic windbags at each corner of it, and outside this are the borders with square panels depicting the routines of the agricultural year, ploughing, sowing, harvest. These cameos of rural life seem to prefigure so much of later traditional Catalan design, especially of tiles. Not surprisingly after 900 years, some of the edges have become worn and are missing. The miracle is that these vivid images of the Christian cosmos have survived so well.

My attempt to search in Girona for Arab influences was centred on the Arab baths. I soon discovered that the name was misleading, for they are certainly not Arab in the sense of dating from the brief occupation of the Arabs, over perhaps sixty years in the eighth century. The model here is the Roman-built baths in North Africa, a model adopted by the Arabs, for whom water and bathing was always the most exquisite of luxuries. Introduced to Spain, it was copied by some of the more enlightened Christian states. Destroyed by the French in 1285, the baths were rebuilt and it is substantially a modern rebuilding of this late thirteenth-century building that greets the visitors who pass down the steps through the Moorish, pointed horse-shoe entrance arch. The first room is the cold bath, a square room with a small octagonal pool and above it an octagonal lantern supported by eight slim columns capped by capitals decorated with vegetable motifs. The practical side of things is dealt with by niches for storing clothes on the south side. From this room the medieval bather would have passed into the tepid bath and thence to the hot bath with its underfloor heating system in the best Roman manner.

I had visited Girona on a number of occasions in the past and been disappointed by it. Dirty, crowded and foul-smelling, the streets around the market littered with rotting vegetables and fruit, its one strong point seemed to be that it was a good transport centre, a place to change buses. All that is now past. Girona is a proud example of the new Catalonia. I was inclined to put a lot of this down to the dynamism of the town council, but local people made it clear to me that there were other factors at work here. The middle-aged man in the post office, a crisp open-neck blue shirt hanging outside the ample waist of his trousers, talked of it as the centre of a flourishing region where industry, agriculture and tourism had all done well in the two decades since I had last changed buses there. A woman in a shoe shop in the *rambla* mentioned 1992, and Girona's position on the motorway and railway to France.

1992, as well as the year of closer European integration, is also the 500th anniversary of the expulsion of the Jews from Spain. In addition, the Jews were one of the many aspects of Spanish history that were offically ignored in Franco's Spain. And so with the transition to democracy, the Jews have found their moment in Girona. Practically the first thing I was offered in the local tourist office on the banks of the river Ter was a booklet in English called *The Jews of Girona*, published by the Girona town council and another called *Catalonia and the Jews* from the Generalitat. Both were dated 1989.

Later, I was able to visit the Centre Isaac el Cec in the old Jewish quarter (the *call*). It is in a steep narrow street closed off for many years but reopened by the town council in 1975. The

53

centre offers a clear and moving audiovisual presentation on the history of the Jews of Girona. Jews arrived as early as AD 400 and by 889, twenty-five Jewish families had taken over the houses of the clergy built in the area south of the cathedral, thus establishing the ghetto, the *call*, a word preserved to this day in street names throughout Catalonia. The location of the ghetto is very significant, in the dark little alleyways off the Carrer de la Força (the route of the Via Augusta) in the very heart of the medieval city. Nothing better reflects the importance of the Jews in the civic and commercial life of Girona. During the Middle Ages the Jews constituted up to seven per cent of the population of Catalonia, with 400 in Girona and up to 4,000 in Barcelona.

Jewish communities, *aljamas*, were legally constituted entities with their synagogues, cemeteries, baths, bakers and butchers. They were governed by their own mayor and aldermen rather than by the town councils. As citizens, the Jews had a unique legal status within feudalism, being the 'property of the king'. They paid royal taxes, but not municipal taxes, and tended to thrive in towns where the royal power was strongest. Jews worked as gold and silversmiths, cobblers and tailors, with workshops both inside and outside the *Call*; Jewish women were in great demand as midwives. Others worked in traditional Jewish occupations as doctors, moneylenders or pawnbrokers, or as tax and rent collectors for the authorities.

There is major academic debate about the cultural and intellectual affiliations of the Catalan Jews. The culture of the original Sephardic Jews (the Jews of the Iberian peninsula) had been profoundly influenced by contact with Arabs. So, just as it was the Arabs who introduced advanced medical practices into Spain, medicine and midwifery were two of the preferred professions of the Catalan Jews. A knowledge of Arabic was kept up by the intellectuals, although Catalan was their 'language of translation' and for many families the only language they knew and used. But from about 1200, the communities were heavily influenced by Jews expelled from Provence who settled in Catalonia. This wave of Jewish refugees brought with them the teachings of the Cabbala, which proposed, in essence, a mystical and anti-rationalist interpretation of the Old Testament. This led to the flowering of Girona as a centre of Jewish culture, especially in the peaceful first half of the thirteenth century. The Cabbalists are best represented in the person of Moses Ben Nahman (or Nahmanides), known in Catalan as Bonstruc ça Porta, born in Girona in 1194, doctor, philosopher, poet and later Grand Rabbi of Catalonia. In his writings he sought to bring out the 'real meaning' of obscure biblical passages and to capture the essence of 'the common flame that illuminates the heart'.

Anti-Semitism, however, was never far away. As early as the eleventh century there had been outbreaks of attacks on Jews, their goods, their homes, their lands and their cemetery. A lethal combination of popular jealousy of what was seen as Jewish privileges and the intolerance of Christian priests was especially effective when it coincided with other motives for popular discontent. In 1263 in Barcelona, Jaume I organised a disputation between Nahmanides and a converted Jew and Dominican friar called Pau Cristià, which centred on the status of Jesus (prophet or Son of God) and whether the Jews were responsible for the death of Jesus. At one level such an intellectual event might be seen as an act of broad-minded tolerance. The gentle philosopher may have won the intellectual debate, but the fanaticism of the friar provided the pivot for a new wave of anti-Semitism, with outbreaks of violence in 1276, 1278 and 1285. In the fourteenth century, the crown, needing the support of the violently anti-Jewish Dominicans, withdrew its support from the Jews for sufficiently long to allow the pogrom of 1348, the immediate cause of which was the accusation that Jews had 'caused' the Black Death. In England such popular agitation climaxed in the Peasants Revolt of 1381. In Spain it culminated in the pogroms of 1391, which began in Seville and spread throughout the peninsula. In Barcelona, a peasant uprising in the Vallès led to a march on the city, where their aggression was deflected by the city authorities against the Jews. The Barcelona Jews never recovered from this attack, and soon afterwards the Consell de Cent (city council) was forced to set up its own financial exchanges at the Llotja (now the Barcelona stock exchange). Although some Christian families in Girona gave shelter to Jewish neighbours, the *call* was ransacked and forty Jews were killed. Eventually the town council was forced to intervene and to shut the remaining Jews into the Torre Gironella, an old Roman fortress tower in the highest part of the town. The figure for conversions for that year (seventy – the usual average was one per year) indicates the extreme pressure on the *aljama*.

The king was now less dependent on Jewish taxes, and the

pressure on the *aljama* continued into the fifteenth century. The Jews were now confined to the *Call*, all the entrances to which but one were sealed off. It was now truly a ghetto. Jews were forbidden to have doors and windows onto the Carrer de la Força, along which Christian processions and funerals passed. In 1445 new regulations were announced including a ban on Jews leaving the *Call* except in the traditional Jewish costume of cloaks and skullcaps. Evangelism continued to stoke the fires of anti-Semitism. It is all too familiar to the modern reader, and it is hard to confront the final expulsion of the Jews in 1492 without tears of anger.

By 1492 the 'Catholic Kings' (Ferdinand and Isabella) were ruling the whole of Spain. The edict coincided with the arrival of Columbus in America. It is immediately obvious, I think, why 1992 is such a difficult year for Spain. Celebration of the 500th anniversary of Columbus' trip cannot ignore that it is also the 500th anniversary of the high point of Spanish anti-Semitism or of the beginning of the process of colonisation in America which led to the death of millions of the native American Indians from disease and war and the destruction of cultures great and small – the Black Legend. Little wonder that the World Fair in Seville and the Olympic Games in Barcelona are the chief targets of national celebrations for that year. The Jews were given two options, expulsion or conversion. Those that stayed became the targets of the Inquisition. For those that went, it was the end of an association with Girona which for some families went back 600 years. The Jews were allowed to sell their goods and property so that at least they did not leave empty-handed. On 31 July, four months after the expulsion order, the last Jews left the *call*.

For 500 years the Jews of Girona have been only a shameful memory. The sadness of the Sephardic diaspora is best represented for me in the gravelly tones of Rosa Zaragoza, a contemporary Catalan folk singer who has set to music the text of medieval Jewish-Catalan wedding songs, written in Catalan but in Hebrew script. In order to write the music she visited Israel and collected tunes from the oral tradition still alive among the distant descendants of those unfortunate Sephardic Jews expelled from the peninsula in 1492.

From the Isaac el Cec centre it is just a few yards to the cathedral. On the next corner, at the foot of a long flight of steps, is a statue by the modern Catalan sculptor, Subirachs. It celebrates the triumph of reason over superstition, the ending, in 1416, of a fifty-year controversy over whether the single nave of the rebuilt cathedral would or would not support the weight of the roof. Girona cathedral is impressive, but certainly not pretty. It speaks of the power of the medieval Church, but also of its intolerance. Coming straight into the cathedral after spending a morning considering the history of Girona's Jews, it also reinforces the notion of a symbiotic relationship between that power and popular ignorance, credulence and superstition. To pass from the nave of Girona cathedral to the tapestry of the Creation in its museum is to retreat to an earlier, more innocent age.

Most Catalan towns of any importance had their Jewish communities. The Barcelona *aljama* of 4,000 people was twice the size of its modern Jewish community, which dates from 1918, but there are few visible remains apart from street names and the name of Montjuïc, the 'Jewish mountain'.

It is more fun, if you are looking for signs of the Jews, to go to Besalú, a town in the foothills of the Pyrenees, thirty-one kilometres from Girona in the volcanic country known as the Garrotxa. It was once the capital of an important county, but its population of 2,000 scarcely justifies even the name of town by English standards. It has many fine buildings in golden stone, including a fortified bridge rebuilt in 1965 after its destruction by the retreating Republican forces in 1939, a hospital and several churches, of which one, the monastic church of Sant Pere, is outstanding. It has three naves and a transept supported by a brilliant cluster of four double columns with richly carved capitals and a passage behind the altar, and represents a more expansive view of the Romanesque than the churches of the Vall de Boí. But it is the Miqwah, the Jewish baths, which are the most valuable relic of the medieval town. The entrance is down a flight of stone steps, but the building has external lighting because it is built onto the steep bank of the river with a view of the magnificent bridge. It was Easter Sunday in Besalú and everything was open, everything free. There were white stocks, carnations and Easter lilies on the altars. After all, the Romans and not the Jews killed Christ and the existence of this ritual bath-house demonstrates how well developed was the life of the Jews in Catalonia. The Miqwah was a small pool of rectangular plan, probably no more than three metres by one metre, supplied by water from a thermal spring and from the river Fluvià. In the sixteenth century it was in use as a dye-house, but in later centuries became buried under earth and mud from river floods. Restoration work began only in 1964. Here, among the volcanic foothills, the snowy peaks of the Pyrenees just creeping into view above them, the Jews found a home before that second diaspora began in 1492.

The Jews were a major factor in the growth of medieval Catalonia, in crafts and professions, and through their roles in finance and public administration. As philosophers and theologians they placed spirituality above dogma and helped to make the nation a more tolerant place than otherwise it might have been.

If Girona and Besalú are the places to dwell on the Jewish contribution to Catalan history, then Lleida turned out to be the place to find evidence of the influence of the Arabs. The early impulse of the reconquest ran out of steam south of Barcelona, after the failure of the attempt to reconquer Tortosa and cross the Ebre (805–9). There is a lengthy gap before the eventual fall of Tortosa in 1148 and of Lleida the following year. The four centuries of Arab rule in these alternating lands of drought and irrigation are hinted at here and there in the survival of a name or the sudden occurrence of Moorish decorative motifs on Christian churches. But there is no Alhambra (Granada), no Giralda (Seville), no mosque (Córdoba), which speaks directly to the traveller of this lost part of the Catalan story, and the offical version of Catalan history put out by the Generalitat simply ignores it.

Lleida is a Roman foundation, but during the Arab period expanded both in terms of population and importance. There appear to have been both Christian and Jewish quarters, further evidence that the simple story of the 'reconquest' is only a half-truth. For long periods, Jews, Christians and Arabs lived side by side in harmony, on both sides of the nominal frontier between Christian and Muslim Spain. In the early eleventh century, after the break-up of the great Caliphate of Córdoba, Lleida became the capital of a *taifa*, or minor kingdom. At the beginning of the next century it fell into the hands of the Almoravides, Saharan tribesmen who performed something of the role of the crusaders, sometimes bravely fighting for the faith, more often spreading violence and chaos and self-seeking as they went.

Lleida is dominated by a great, flat hill above the orchards of the Segre valley, the narrow streets of the old town, and the spreading modern suburbs. That hill, in turn, is dominated by the outline of the Seu Vella, the old cathedral. The hilltop is the site of the Arab fortress of Suda, and as so often in Spain, there is direct continuity from one culture to another. In 1300 the Estudi General was opened and for many years was the only university in the Aragonese-Catalan kingdom. Lleida's decline began early, exacerbated by the expulsion of the Jews in 1492. Each subsequent revival ended in violence, reflecting the key strategic role of Lleida as the great fortress of these border lands. Lleida was besieged three times in the 1640s during the War of the Harvesters (Els Segadors), and much of the old town was demolished after the end of the War of the Spanish Succession in 1714. So the Arab fortress of Suda became a Bourbon fortress. A gunpowder explosion during the Napoleonic Wars put paid to the castle and a whole suburb. And so it goes on. The 1900 population of 1,000 was less than in 1400. Yet againt the odds, Lleida is today a thriving town of 100,000 with successful industries based on agriculture, engineering and transport, less dependent on tourism than the coastal regions but keen to encourage more visitors to sample its pleasures, which range from the city itself and the other towns of the plains (Balaguer, Agramunt) to the wild national parks of the high Pyrenees and the ski resorts of the Vall d'Aran. Its new tourist office in the Edifici Pal·las, a newly converted art-nouveau house, has a modern façade on the Paeria, the open pedestrianised precinct at the heart of Lleida's civic life, as well as the splendid façade facing the river, with long, slim, stone columns linking the outside of the balconies and the windows creating a second plane behind.

There is major reconstruction going on in the vicinity of Castle Hill and the Seu Vella. It is an attempt to emphasise its status as a Bourbon fortress and to link it to that period of Catalan history at the beginning of the eighteenth century when the nation's traditional rights and institutions were swept away. The arms of Spain have been replaced above the gateway. But there are peaceful gardens and walkways here, and like the monumental parts of Tarragona, it is a popular place for older people to sit and talk and enjoy the spring sunshine. To me their faces show a contentment with their lives and experiences, calm faces very different from the ones I am used to seeing every day in the crush and rush of London streets.

The Seu Vella, the old cathedral, begun in 1203 and consecrated in 1278, is no longer in use as a church. I share the climb with joggers and teenagers learning to ride those dangerous mopeds still so popular in France, Italy and Spain. The view alone is worth the exertion, from the cluttered roofs of the old town, those parts which have survived Lleida's tumultuous history, almost immediately below, to the modern blocks of flats in the suburbs. And industry, too, and the river, before the fields which extend across the plains in all directions as far as the eye can see. Turning away from the main spread of the city, which is south and east, the snowy peaks of the Pyrenees are just peeping over the horizon to the north. As the cathedral is no longer in use as a church, there is an admission charge, and the clever doorkeeper manages to smoke, listen to music on his portable radio and wash the floor in-between collecting money – he clearly feels that the No Smoking signs refer only to visitors.

After the 1707 siege, the cathedral, along with the remains of the surrounding houses, was occupied by the military and the whole area rebuilt as a fortress. The cathedral was subsequently used as a warehouse, prison, military quarters and hospital. A new neoclassical cathedral was built between 1761 and 1781 at the foot of the hill. In 1949 reconstruction work began on the Seu Vella to remove the many changes made since 1707, which included an inner roof, the division of the nave into rooms and the opening up of new doorways.

For a building with such a bizarre history, it is remarkable how much there is still to see and admire, especially in the many chapels. In the chapel of Sant Tomàs are thirteenth-century wall paintings in the upper part and tympanum, but more remarkable are the intertwined patterns of the abstract Mudejar paintings on the lower walls. Mudejar refers to the work of Moorish craftsmen who continued to live in Christian Spain, just as Mozarab refers to the work of Christians who lived in Muslim areas. In both cases, the craftsmen developed styles which show the influences of both cultures. Abstract design has always existed in Western culture, but the Mudejar work at the Seu Vella in Lleida marks a clear break with the moralising, storytelling tradition of the Romanesque. Over three-quarters of all the capitals at Lleida are purely decorative. The external doorways of the cathedral are also excellent examples of the Lleida school of stonemasons whose influence was to spread as far away as Valencia cathedral.

The values of medieval craftsmanship are constant, but the design idiom of Lleida is unique.

The most magnificent spot in the Seu Vella is the cloister. Cloisters are traditionally secluded, intimate places. But not at Lleida. The cloister is placed in front of the building, like the narthex of a basilica, and covers every period of Catalan Gothic from the transition from Romanesque to the most florid Gothic ornament. Its proportions are monumental, and situated as it is in front of the church and on the edge of the hill, there are splendid views on the open south side through the open cloister tracery to the surrounding countryside. I do not know of any comparable structure. Yet some of the special attractions of cloisters are here, not least the slanting evening sunshine across the top of the cloisters lighting up the rich orange-brown stone. The distinctiveness of this Lleida style seems to come from the union of three elements: abstract, intertwining forms from the Islamic tradition, with its refusal to countenance representational art; vegetable forms of leaves and fruit; birds and animals and figures from the older European tradition of the Romanesque. It is the sheer scale and height and grandeur that impresses most; it makes Tarragona's cloister, perfect in its own way, seem poky indeed.

But the grand finale of this union of east and west, Christianity and Islam, is the great west porch of the parish church of the little town of Agramunt. I was lucky to arrive at Agramunt not knowing what to expect, lucky that it was market day, that the sun was shining, that the first strawberries from the south had arrived on the market. The market crowds along the arcaded streets in the centre of the town and spreads across the open area in front of the west façade of the church. So to see the porch for the first time, I had to strain across market stalls piled high with plants, and pots and pans, clothes and fruit and vegetables, and Moroccans selling transistor radios and rugs and carpets. A metaphor often used in art criticism is that of a particular work being 'alive'. Well, this porch is alive, with the bustle of the town matched by the dozens of martins whose nests (I counted well over one hundred) are thickly encrusted around the vaults of the porch. And no-one seems to want to move them. They were still there, swooping to feed their clamouring young in the still golden light of a July evening. This time there was no market, but a swarm of young cyclists were rapidly marshalled to act as 'foreground' for the photo I had promised myself.

61

This great porch has a familiar aura for those who know and love the great wool churches of Suffolk. It was paid for by the weavers guild, and to this day Agramunt remains a town that lives from and with the land, its only industries being those connected with farm machinery or the processing of food. The porch was built in 1283, itself a surprising fact for it is clearly semicircular, and although people better qualified than I might detect elements of transition from Romanesque to Gothic, Gothic it clearly is not. It is the perfect combination of East and West, of representational art and abstraction, of animal and vegetable, of the divine and the human. Each archivolt has a character of its own, whether it is the figures of saints, or abstract patterning. In the centre of the arches above the door is a scene of the Adoration of the Virgin Mary with her attendants either side, set in a wide arch flat to the wall with a marvellously intricate, trellis-work frieze. The columns are slim and graceful with delicate inter-twined foliage in the capitals.

Caught up with the hectic life of Girona and Barcelona, it was some time before I entirely came to terms with Lleida. During two years of living in Barcelona, it had not been part of 'my' Catalonia. But when I went to visit my old friends in Vilanova i La Geltrú, between Barcelona and Tarragona, it became clear to me that I was on the verge of an important development in my own thinking about the country. It was not enough to see Lleida as a land of transition, of battle and fortified villages. Lleida had its own ways, its own traditions, and I began to think of Catalonia as more complex culturally than I had bfore. In Vilanova people talked to me at length about 'old' and 'new' Catalonia, the 'old' being the early medieval counties north of a line from the rocky outcrops of the Garraf cliffs (between Barcelona airport and Sitges) and the Ribagorça in the high mountains above Lleida. South of this line lay the lands that had continued to be under Arab control for another 300 years stretching from Lleida to Vilanova and south down the coast to the Ebre delta in a great triangle.

The *sardana* is often described as the national dance of Cata-lonia. But Xavier Orriols, a friendly, talkative Vilanova musicolo-gist and expert on popular culture, identified the *sardana* as a regional dance, the dance above all of the Empordà, the area between Girona, Figueres and the Costa Brava. He regretted the way that the music of the traditional *cobla* band, which plays the *sardana* music, had become stagnant and limited by the demands of the dance itself, which has a high degree of formality about it. Yet he recognised that the *sardana*, with its obvious symbolism of the dancers holding hands in a circle, had been taken up by the cultural nationalists at the turn of the century, and also by the *noucentista* artists, for whom it was another expression of the essence of the Mediterranean world. From there to the mind of the President of the present Generalitat is a small step! Xavier and his friends were interested in the older instruments from which the *cobla* had developed, the bagpipes and the shawm, a simple double-reed wind instrument once common throughout Europe. These instruments in turn could be used to accompany a whole variety of popular cultural events.

These arguments will be taken up again in the chapter on popular culture. I wanted to rehearse them here because they point to some of the dangers which are just as implicit in the nationalism of small nations as that of large nations. It is a tendency for certain cultural forms, certain traditions, certain groups within the population, to claim a monopoly over the identity of a particular nation (whether nation state or nation without a state matters little here). In medieval Catalonia, the complex relationships of Jewish, Moorish and Christian culture twine around one another like the decoration of the porch at Agramunt. The cultures of modern Catalonia are many and varied, popular, classical, local and international. No Catalan can ignore the existence of large numbers of people born in Catalonia but whose parents or grandparents have come from other parts of Spain. Or of other newcomers from Morocco or other Western European countries. Catalonia today is again what it was in the Middle Ages, a multiethnic, multiracial, multicultural society.

All this makes the task of building a nation more difficult but more exciting too, and ultimately will contribute something to a world in which every culture is seen to have its place and its coherence. There are many lessons of 1492–1992. But for Catalonia one stands out from all the rest. It is not the chauvinism of 1492, the enforced unity, that is a model for the new Spain, but those moments of harmony which occurred more often than we tend to think during the Middle Ages when Christians, Jews and Muslims valued and shared their learning and their cultures.

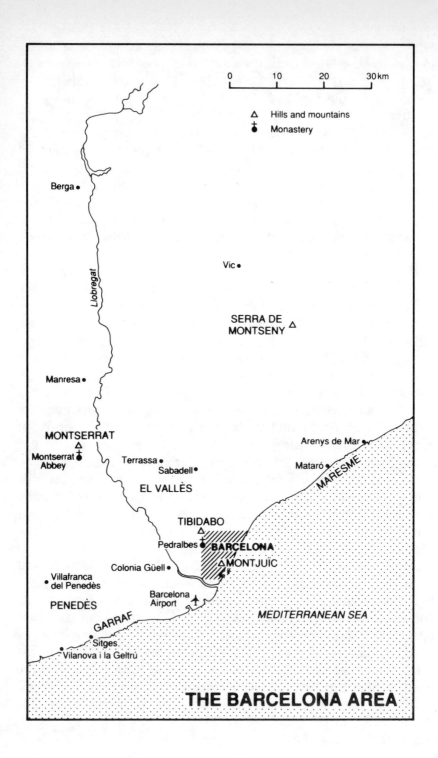

THE BARCELONA AREA

Chapter 6

Ruling the Waves

The medieval Catalan empire was an extraordinary affair. It was ruled not in the name of Catalonia, but in the name of Aragon (with its capital at Saragossa). The marriage of the Count of Barcelona and the Queen of Aragon in 1137 had united the two regional powers and led almost directly to the reconquest of Tortosa and Lleida from the Arabs, both completed by the middle of the century. Previously, the county of Barcelona had aimed at extending Catalan influence north of the Pyrenees in what is now France. However, this brought the Catalans into conflict with wider European concerns such as the rivalry between the English and French crowns for the control of the lands of southern France. After the defeat of Pere (Peter) I at Muret in 1213 by an army led by Simon de Montfort, this policy was reversed.

From now on, the Catalans would concentrate on spreading their influence south along the coast of Spain and east across the Mediterranean. Jaume (James) I conquered Majorca from the Arabs in 1229 and the kingdom of Valencia in 1238. Later in the thirteenth century, Sardinia and Sicily fell under Catalan control. In the case of Sicily this followed the Sicilian Vespers uprising against the French King Charles I who ruled Naples in mainland Italy. Early in the fourteenth century Catalan pirates attacked the Byzantine empire and for many years controlled the duchy of Athens. As late as the fifteenth century, when Castilian influence had already become strong in a Catalonia weakened by internal division, plague and depopulation, Alfons the Magnanimous conquered Naples, where he remained to rule over one of the great humanist courts of early Renaissance Europe.

The political and commercial history of the medieval Catalans takes literary form in the chronicles of Ramon Muntaner. Muntaner was born in the town of Perelada in the Empordà, and accompanied numerous Catalan expeditions, including those to Greece. He had first-hand experience of the events he describes and spent the last years of his life (he died in 1336) writing in fulsome terms of the brave exploits of his heroes. There is no mistaking the pride Muntaner takes in his work and in the language, repeatedly telling us of far-off places where the 'natives' speak the 'fairest Catalan in the world'. The fairest, the richest, the wisest, there is no end to Muntaner's superlatives.

However, more serious readings of history reveal the Catalan expeditionaries to have been little more than pirates and free-booters, like Drake and Raleigh. Heroes of a kind, but more inclined to pride and lust and greed than to courtly behaviour in the name of their sovereigns. While Muntaner does not narrate events in these terms, there is evidence of this in the chronicle. For example, the pirate admiral Roger de Lauria is in Barcelona with fifty days to spare before attending the coronation of King Alfons II in Saragossa. He begs leave of the King to go on a raiding expedition up the French coast rather than 'leaving my galley crews to get into trouble round here'. The King agrees, and off goes the noble admiral to sack a few French towns. One particular town is sacked and burned to the ground 'except for the church, which is very pretty', a typical example of Muntaner's unintentional humour. Leaving his galleys at Tortosa in charge of his nephew Joan (John), Roger suggests that he should raid Moorish lands, 'as long as they haven't signed a peace treaty with the King' and 'try and win some booty for the galleys so that the crews will be kept happy'.

This territorial expansion was not just about the wealth of kings and the freebooting activities of pirates. It was also about Barcelona, and the power of Barcelona merchants and bankers who were the main beneficiaries of expansion. Trade, as ever, was the motor of conquest. In some cases, conquest confirmed existing trading links, in others it created fresh opportunities. This trade was regulated by consulates in all the major Mediterranean towns, and by the code of commercial and maritime practice consolidated in the mid-fourteenth century in the *Llibre del Consolat del Mar* (the Maritime Consulate Book). It is the first book of its kind and was translated and adopted as standard practice by the other Mediterranean powers. By 1335 there were five consuls and seventeen vice-consuls spread as far away as Flanders, Venice, Byzantium and Beirut, where Catalan traders, including Catalan Jews, competed with Venetians and Genoese for trade.

The church of Santa Maria del Mar (Our Lady of the Sea) in Barcelona, like the great London town churches, is a church which is both very special but also very ordinary in the sense that it becomes part of your daily life and experience. I used it frequently as a short cut to and from the main railway terminus, the Estació de França, rushing through when hurrying to catch a train or perhaps pausing for a few moments on a Sunday evening to admire the coloured lights from the west rose window on the bare stone of the octagonal pillars on the way back from an excursion to the country.

Santa Maria is located right on the fringe of Barcelona's 'Gothic Quarter', nearer the old stock exchange and central market and the port than it is to the Plaça San Jaume or the cathedral, because that is the sort of church it has always been. A church for lovers' meetings, for commercial plots, for great public occasions such as the blessing of expeditionary fleets, rather than for individual religious experience. It is also Catalan Gothic at its most extrovert, an exercise in pure space supported only by the internal buttresses that divide off the side-chapels, and the slim octagonal pillars which crowd like forest pines around a glade at the east end. The building of Santa Maria lasted from 1329 to 1384 and it represents both the culmination of Catalan Gothic and the high point of Barcelona's commercial empire. The three high naves divided only by the slimmest of columns made it the perfect church for civic ceremony. Unfortunately, no pictures exist of this, and the only way to imagine it is perhaps through the Dutch pictures of the seventeenth century, where the churches are represented as part of the fabric of commercial town life.

When the Civil War broke out in 1936, anarchist, Trotskyite and communist gangs burned many of the churches in Barcelona. Unlike the cathedral, Santa Maria was not spared by the incendiaries, and until very recently the roof still carried the scars where furnishings, altars and pews were heaped together and set alight. Like so much else in the Civil War, it was swift and terrible revenge for what the working class saw as centuries of simmering injustice. The left burned churches in 1936 as the liberals had burned the monasteries in the 1830s. The Church was seen as part of the Spanish Establishment which had plotted the military uprising of Franco, who described his revolt as a 'crusade'.

Above all, Santa Maria is the church of the graceful octagonal towers, the slimmest I know, rising magically from the gloomy depths of the Argenteria (Silversmiths) street as you come down from the cathedral across the bustle of the modern Via Layetana. The silversmiths have gone but the herbalists still ply their trade in the little shops on either side of the street. Originally this street led straight to the sea, but in the centuries following the building of Santa Maria on the seafront, the sea was driven back to the position of the present port and sordid alleys grew up between the church and the sea. But Santa Maria has always been the church of the sea and of the people who live from it – fishermen and sailors, traders and merchants. A flower seller still occupies the porch at the eastern end of the church, although she no longer looks down on the bustle outside the Born market, which is now closed and awaiting redevelopment. The towers show up above the surrounding buildings from the port, and can be picked out easily from the heights of Tibidabo or Montjuïc, the hills above Barcelona. The church sits within the city, which flows on around it. Nothing in our acquisitive, materialistic society is likely to shock it. Santa Maria represents that other world of creativity and beauty which begins when the struggle for day-to-day survival leaves off. Its grace and space were to the medieval merchant economy what *Modernisme* (art nouveau) was for the Catalans of the Industrial Revolution, the beauty that was missing from their hectic everyday pursuit of wealth.

Santa Maria is not the only building in Barcelona where the spirit of Catalonia's imperial past is palpable. Another is the Llotja (stock exchange) in the same district down by the port. It dates from about 1360, when it was established as the base for Catalan traders and consuls, but externally it is undistinguished neoclassical architecture from the early days of Barcelona's nineteenth-century resurrection as a great industrial and commercial centre. The greatest accomplishment of its architects was to preserve the medieval transactions room intact, and it is one of a number of civil Gothic buildings which are more characteristic of Barcelona Gothic than the religious buildings. The Llotja stands at one end of the great avenue which, given modern traffic conditions, has effectively severed Barcelona from the port and the sea. One of the projects of the new urbanism is to revive this area as a proper esplanade, reuniting city and port. But if you can forget for a moment the continual snarl of car and lorry engines, the exhaust fumes and the blaring of horns, the view is still among the best loved in the city, with the statue of Columbus at the foot of the *rambla* and the abrupt cliff face of Montjuïc behind. Columbus points out to sea, towards his native Italy and the lands of the Catalan empire rather than towards the New World. It is a rich emblem of Barcelona's past.

Just beyond Columbus, and the chaotic roadworks, where traffic is being organised into underground carriageways which will facilitate the surface developments of Barcelona's new 'prom', are the old royal shipyards – the Drassanes. Begun in 1275 it consists of great naves with pointed arches. Here the ships that maintained Catalan supremacy in the Mediterranean were built and repaired. It is now the maritime museum. Extensive works are underway here at the time of writing (1990). There are plans to revive the popular festivities associated with the sea, as well as the use of the port for sporting activities, with new beaches and pleasure marinas along a five-kilometre stretch of coast.

On the left (Montjuïc) side of the *rambla* going up towards the Plaça de Catalunya is the Hospital of the Holy Cross, begun in 1403. At this period, the whole area left of the *rambla* was enclosed by a wall, and this area of the Raval, with its monasteries and market gardens, brought firmly within the scope of the city authorities. At the same time, the *rambla* itself was retained as an open space for processions and other city events, a role it has maintained ever since. The hospital remains an oasis of peace in a crowded city, with its quiet sandy courtyards and orange trees. It houses the National Library and also the Institute of Catalan Studies. Outside is Barcelona's statue to Sir Alexander Fleming, long a cult figure in Catalonia and Spain. He is seldom without flowers from his well-wishers, traditionally reckoned to be the prostitutes of the nearby Barri Xinès (Chinese Quarter, though with no obvious Chinese connection) and no doubt their customers. And if flowers are missing, his head and the bowl of the fountain in front of him are equally popular with the local pigeons and sparrows. Writing in 1953, Langdon-Davies also confirmed the reverence for Fleming in Barcelona. He told the story of the eightieth birthday celebration of the oldest flower seller in the *rambla*. She was able to remember occasions when royalty and aristocrats had bought bouquets and buttonholes, but her proudest moment, the one she treasured most, had been the day that

Fleming had stopped at her stall, for his penicillin had saved the life of her dearest friend.

The Barri Xinès is a typical international sailors' quarter, given over to heavy drinking and prostitution of the most varied kinds. Narrow, dingy, miserable, overcrowded, sordid are all words that come to mind if you venture down the streets to the left of the *rambla*. Years ago, the area had its attraction for local people looking for cheap excitement, but in the new liberal atmosphere of Catalonia there are more pleasant areas of town in which to seek pleasure. In a country where little is now forbidden, there is little to shock or excite the average Catalan in these narrow streets. My students used to take me years ago to the Bar London in the Carrer Nou de la Rambla, and this is still a pleasant nightspot in an area dominated by sex shops and amusement arcades, a café that livens up when the theatres shut in the early hours of the morning. In the 1920s it was where agents and impresarios went to sign up circus acts, and it retains this strong link with the world of popular entertainment.

So far I have scarcely mentioned the Gothic Quarter itself, the area to the right of the *rambla*, between the cathedral and the sea. Here, as part of the royal palace, is the Tinell room. The aim was to impress – a place where visiting princes and ambassadors could be received, or public meetings held, in a setting which spoke of the grandeur of the Aragonese-Catalan court. The room is typical of Barcelona civic Gothic, a vast hall 30 metres long and 15 metres wide with great stone diaphragm arches. This whole complex of the royal palace, with its royal chapel of Santa Àgata and the curious watchtower, is built into and above the old Roman wall on the east side of the old town. They open onto an almost enclosed open space – the Plaça del Rei (King's Square) – which despite its royal name, Oriol Bohigas, Barcelona architect and town planner, has called a 'Republican' open space at the heart of medieval Catalan democracy. It is now a popular venue in summer for concerts and plays of all kinds. The civil authorities of Barcelona had their own equally impressive Gothic hall – the Sala de Cent – where the town council (the Consell de Cent, or Council of a Hundred) met. As at the stock exchange, Gothic lurks behind a neoclassical façade, though an older decorative Gothic façade can still be seen down a side street – the Carrer de la Cuitat.

The literary output of medieval Catalonia starts rather later than the political and commercial expansion. Part of the reason for this is the intense traffic between Catalonia and Provence. In the twelfth and thirteenth centuries, Catalan poets wrote in the fashionable language of the Provençal troubadours. The contemporary Majorcan singer Maria del Mar Bonet has recorded works by the Provençal troubadours in her 'Breviari d'Amor' ('The Epitome of Love') album. Catalan literature came of age not on the mainland but on the island of Majorca with the work of the philosopher and mystic Ramon Llull (Raymond Lully). Llull lived from 1233 to 1315 and was a man of enormous learning and energy. His first book, written in Arabic (which he knew better than Latin) is supposed to have been one million words long. His work became well known all over Europe and the *Book of the Order of Chivalry* was printed in an English translation by Caxton. The best-known Catalan poets, Jordi de Sant Jordi and Ausiàs March, date from the first half of the fifteenth century when, in retrospect, the Catalan decline had already begun. Both came from Valencia. Love, death and morality were their themes, and they helped to bring into Spain the influence of the first Italian Renaissance – the works of Petrarch and Dante. March was obsessed by death beyond the requirements of poetic convention. Love is fleeting and must end in unhappiness. The law of life is solitude, deprivation, sickness and death.

None of these three writers came from Catalonia. For a short period in the Middle Ages, Catalan became an international language, and it remains the language of Valencia, the Balearic Islands and a corner of France. This idea of the 'Catalan lands' is still very much alive, of a historic homeland of the Catalan-speaking people. Clearly countries with a common language and some shared history will be inclined to have good relations with one another. The UK-USA relationship or the Commonwealth are good examples of this. But dig deeper, and you find domination as often as partnership. Within a federal Spain, the Valencians and the islanders have their statutes of autonomy which are highly valued. And there is little evidence that they want to enter into a federation with Catalonia outside the Spanish context, a federation that would certainly be dominated by Catalonia in general and Barcelona in particular. The linguistic and cultural links are real enough, but mindless patriotism is not a Catalan trait of character, and the economic argument for Catalan autonomy has always outweighed the emotional appeal of a 'Greater Catalonia'.

An essential tool used by the Catalan crown in the development of the lands of New Catalonia was monasticism. Immediately after the reconquest of the Ebre valley in the twelfth century, Ramon Berenguer IV moved to grant the Cistercians lands in the new territories. This was the origin of the three great foundations of Poblet, Santes Creus and Vallbona de les Monges. Despite the aim of the Cistercians to have done with corruption and the lure of wordly wealth, these monasteries must be understood not just as religious organisations but as units of social and economic organisation under royal patronage. In earlier centuries, the Benedictines at Ripoll and Sant Pere de Rodes had placed great emphasis on teaching and preaching. The Cistercians looked at the foundation of new abbeys as economic investments, which also benefited the civic authorities keen to consolidate their hold on the new lands. So at Vallbona on the edge of the Lleida plain, the nuns drained the marshy valley and set up farms and villages. As you approach Poblet on the Francolí river the immediate impression is of a rich, fertile country with vines, fruit and corn growing in abundance. At its peak, Poblet had jurisdiction over seven baronies, owned sixty villages and appointed the mayors of ten towns. A French visitor in 1316 reported that the monastery owned 53 mules, 40 horses, 1,100 calves, 1,215 sheep, 1,500 goats and 162 pigs. Santes Creus lies, like Poblet, invitingly close to the motorway from Barcelona to Lleida and beyond, and its feudal powers extended widely in the rich olive and vine-growing country of the Penedès and the lowlands inland from Tarragona.

My own contact with Poblet dates back to the days when I used to spend weekends in Tarragona with a music teacher who was very friendly with the organist at the monastery. So several times on Sunday afternoons we drove up through the rather cheerless winter landscape of grey-green olives and black vine stumps to spend the afternoon in the organ loft. The monks are friendly and well informed, both about the history of which they are custodians and also events in the wider world. This has never been a place shut off from the world. Poblet and Santes Creus were the preferred places of death for the Catalan kings, and some of the finest monuments are the tombs of the kings, under their elaborate Gothic canopies. Yet neither place reaches the austere solemnity of El Escorial, the great pantheon of the Castilian kings in the Guadarrama mountains northwest of Madrid. There is always an airy lightness to this New Catalonia

Gothic, a celebration of life more than a meditation on death, a sensuality which matches the pleasure-loving nature of Mediterranean cultures.

Today, these old monasteries are more places for excursion than for serious pilgrimage. There is not the religious or nationalist fervour here that there is at Montserrat, no equivalent of the Sunday morning mass at Montserrat when Catalans from all over gather to sing the words of the *Virolai*, the national hymn of Catalonia to words by the poet Verdaguer. Montserrat, high above the Llobregat valley, wedged securely between great rounded rocky outcrops which rise to 1,200 metres, is the centre of pilgrimage in Catalonia. The Romanesque statue of the Black Virgin is supposed to possess miraculous powers, and Montserrat (shortened to Montse) is still one of the most popular names for Catalan women. The Benedictine community of seventy-five monks, with their own printing press, have identified themselves very closely with the cause of Catalan nationalism, so much so that Abbot Escarré was eventually exiled at the end of 1963 for his open criticism of the Franco regime: 'The regime of General Franco calls itself Christian, but fails to obey the basic principles of Christianity. Catalans have a right to their own culture, history and customs.'

Tortosa cathedral is the apotheosis of this new attitude to Gothic. Tortosa gives itself only slowly to the visitor, with dull, dusty suburbs stretching out along the road towards Tarragona, which is where most visitors arrive from. It owes its existence to having commanded for centuries the lowest crossing of the Ebre. That is no longer the case. The main road crosses the Ebre by an elegant early twentieth-century suspension bridge down at Amposta on the edge of the delta and the motorway crosses nearby. And the trade on the Ebre river ground to a halt in the eighteenth century with the silting up of the delta. So Tortosa has a shabby old-fashioned look about it almost unique among Catalan cities. Yet once through the suburbs, Tortosa shyly begins to show off its charms – art nouveau first, then Renaissance and finally Gothic.

The best way to visit Tortosa is to head straight for the state-run hotel, the *parador*, which sits in the castle overlooking Tortosa. It is a splendid site, high above the city and the green Ebre snaking its way inland between bare, cruel mountains – the badlands of Catalonia. This hotel has been successively Iberian and Roman settlements Arab fort and a Catalan royal palace. But from here you look straight down upon the cathedral and its network of flying buttresses and pinnacles which are unique in Catalonia. It reveals its structure at once, a nave with two aisles and a double ambulatory. Then you can climb down easily towards it, picking your way between little houses and big cactuses to enter eventually through an archway into the cloister and then into the main church.

Inside the cathedral is one outstanding work of art – the retable of the main altar, painted wood in an Italianate style, telling the life history of the Virgin Mary. The Virgin and Child are the centrepiece of the altar but the story flows on around this central image. In a series of panels and scenes, the altar tells of the annunciation and the birth with all those precious details which even the least religious will remember from school carol services – the shepherds in the fields, the child and his parents in the stable with the farm animals and the angels, who seem just as real as any of the other lifelike figures in the scene. From the ambulatory it is also possible to inspect the reverse of the retable. If the scenes that face the congregation are the light and optimistic view of life, here all is darkness and pessimism: Jesus betrayed by a kiss, a symbol of affection turned into a symbol of betrayal, the crucifixion and the empty tomb that spells hope in even the darkest anguish. It is one of those works of art that makes you want desperately to believe, an experience as moving in its own way as Sunday morning mass among the fervent pilgrims at Montserrat.

Yet religion in Tortosa is not a simple matter. A service is taking place in an extraordinary, profligate chapel at the west end of the church, and speaks a very different message from the elegant simplicity of the altarpiece. The church has the power to damn or to save, and individual religious experience is both unnecessary and dangerous to the unity of the church.

And a few yards away on a small island in the middle of the Ebre is a monument 'to those who found glory in the battle of the Ebre', one of the bloodiest of the whole Civil War. What glory? The enemy was their own people, driven to take part in a three-year war. I found it extraordinary that the people of Tortosa could carry on accepting a monument inaugurated by the victor in the war, General Franco. At very least could it not be re-inaugurated as a proper tribute to all those (and not just

Spaniards) who died in the battle of the Ebre? There are moments, as Cela found, when the traveller is filled with a hopeless pessimism at the folly of mankind. This is a sombre spot, with the town and its bridges downstream and the Ebre winding its way northwards into those bare and uncompromising mountains.

For the traveller in a hurry who loves art more than places, there is no doubt that the Museu d'Art de Catalunya in Barcelona is the place to discover the variety and beauty of Catalan Gothic. Here the traveller as art lover can trace the successive influences from other countries which mark out the development of Catalan Gothic. Although religious works continue to be the most numerous subjects, there is also a rich variety of subject matter. From the thirteenth century there are the murals from the Aguilar Palace, one of the aristocratic homes of Barcelona's Montcada street, and which by an extraordinary coincidence now houses the Picasso museum. This depicts in lively detail the conquest of Majorca already referred to. The familiar religious stories are now told with a wealth of everyday detail not found in the Romanesque, which seems a constricted style by contrast. There are successive influences from France, from Italy (especially clear in the work of the Serra family) and from Flanders, culminating in the great fifteenth-century realists Lluís Dalmau and Jaume Huguet. Pere Serra was active in Barcelona in the second half of the fourteenth century. His Virgin, Child and angels from the Convent of St Clare in Tortosa is a work of rare beauty. The Virgin's blue robe is embroidered with a repeated, golden bird motif, and the Child holds a goldfinch in his hand. The bird symbolises the divine spirit in all of us, while the angelic musicians demonstrate how that spirit is expressed in art.

I would recommend just two visits from Barcelona in search of Catalan Gothic painting, one a mere bus ride away at Pedralbes high above the city centre, the other a train journey to the busy textiles town of Manresa, the last outpost of the old suburban railway network. At Pedralbes you either freeze or fry. I have been there in winter when the wind whips down from the bare hills marking the inland limit of the city, reminding you of the fickleness of the Catalan climate, caught between fierce winds from the mountains and gentle breezes from the distant shores of Africa. If the *Tramuntana* blows fiercely enough in winter, it can even snow in Barcelona. But in July and August, Barcelona can become a cauldron, with high levels of humidity and pollution trapped between the sea and the surrounding hills. On my last visit, the old monastery lay sun-bleached and shipwrecked in front of its dusty little square. 'The writer without a pen,' the doorman informed me, as I hunted in my pocket for something to write with, 'is like a smith without a hammer.' It was good to be reminded that writing is a craft like any other, and certainly that particular morning I sweated about my task just as much as the builders repairing the roof of the cloister.

Pedralbes is quite different from other Catalan monasteries, established by nuns who followed the gentle teachings of St Clare and St Francis. The visitor enters through the cloisters and almost immediately comes to the chapel of Saint Michael with its murals by Ferrer Bassa. Little is known about him except that he was active betwen 1324 and 1348 and that he was greatly influenced by Italian painters – Giotto and the Lorenzetti brothers. The colours are fading and there is some chipping of the surface. The subjects are traditional – the Joys of Our Lady, the Life of Christ, figures of saints – but the treatment is lively and at times humorous. Ferrer Bassa also had the occasional problem with perspective that afflicted the early Italians too. So there is a porch above a stable in a Birth of Christ scene which appears to be in the process of being blown up into the air by a gale. But there is real human drama in the Betrayal in the Garden and formal beauty of composition in the burial and annunciation scenes. When I lived in Barcelona, the chapel could only be visited between twelve and two on a Sunday, but the town hall has hammered out an agreement with the nuns which has gradually made most of this complex of buildings open to the visitor, while the nuns have been rehoused in a more modern building close by. The chapter house, the kitchens, which boast equipment from the medieval to the modern, and the hospital wing all help to give an impression of the busy life of a small convent of this kind. The nuns were very interested in herbalism, always a feature of Catalonia, and herbs are still grown in the cloister garden alongside more decorative fir trees, orange trees and fuchsias.

From Pedralbes it is a short, dusty walk to the atmospheric old centre of Sarrià, a village long ago absorbed into Barcelona but which has never entirely lost its village atmosphere. Here I used to come on Sunday afternoons many years ago to play table tennis and to talk politics, and to my delight I found that the same barman still runs the same café in the square, and still serves the same fat sandwiches of Spanish omelette and the same cold, gassy beer.

'Has Sarrià changed?'

'There are more cars, but Sarrià hasn't changed. Not like Barcelona – that's a different city now from twenty years ago!'

'Better?'

'Different.'

The café is as seedy as twenty years ago, the sort of place to postpone indefinitely thinking about a career and the future, or becoming what others expect us to be, and to live life one day at a time. I talk to a young English teacher from County Durham who is doing exactly what I was doing twenty years ago. I wonder what we will both be doing in another twenty years, and if Sarrià will still have that same lazy, timeless feeling which evaporates so completely as you descend back towards the city and are reabsorbed into the hectic pace of Barcelona.

Manresa is an odd town. It is also a town to get lost in. Built on a series of small hills and abrupt valleys on the steep banks of the Cardener river just before it enters the Llobregat, it is frankly disorientating. The most important building is the Seu (cathedral) in a green setting at the highest point of the town. It has an enormous west porch with views of the railway station in the valley beneath, blocks of flats, rocky hillsides, as confused a townscape as you will find anywhere in Catalonia. Like Girona, the cathedral is an expansive building of wide open spaces. Its greatest treasure is the retable of the Holy Spirit by Pere Serra, an immense work of glittering gold and red and blue and green which has been resited in the nave of the church. It dates from 1393/4 and was paid for by the tanners guild. Unfortunately the lower panels are missing and have been replaced by Lluís Borrassà's panels of the Burial of Christ, paid for in 1411 by the shoemakers guild. They are immensely rich paintings full of carefully delineated figures, and it is curious to reflect that these great works of the Catalan Gothic coincided with a period of agrarian discontent and plagues. Something of the answer is suggested by the fact that these works were financed by the local craft guilds. The old feudal order was passing, and the towns and cities of Catalonia acquiring much more importance.

The weather can be equally treacherous in summer as in winter in Catalonia. It was August, only a few weeks after that hot, dusty morning in Pedralbes, yet the rain beat down incessantly all morning on the glistening cobbles of Manresa. From the chilly, dark interior of the church, each of three open doors revealed rectangles of bright green grass, and I needed a torch to bring out the full impact of the paintings. There is much fine stained glass at Manresa, and the windows shone brightly but without penetrating the gloom at ground level. Outside, the river flowed swiftly, its waters turned a rich red by the mud it was carrying from the surrounding fields. All is flux and change and only art, occasionally, endures.

Chapter 7

No More Pyrenees

Il n'y a plus de Pyrénées

(Louis xiv of France in 1700 on the
accession of his grandson to the Spanish throne).

Like many of the students of my generation, I regarded hitchhiking as the only way to travel. I took a lift from Tours in France to Seville in March 1965. With the Pyrenees looming ahead of us, we ran out of petrol halfway up the French side of the Samport pass, far to the west of Catalonia. As the only person in the car who spoke Spanish, I was deputed to hike across the frontier and come back with petrol. The first vehicle to pass was a French police jeep with the men going up to change the guard at the frontier post. A quarter of an hour later I was standing a few yards from Spain in a thick mist through which the only thing that could be seen were enormous banks of dirty snow on either side of a track recently cleared across the summit of the pass.

Moments later a voice shouted at me in French through the mist.

'Hey, you, come over here.'

'Yes, what?'

'We can sell you some petrol. Only a little, mind.'

The police had evidently decided to have pity on me, and proceeded not only to sell me some petrol but to take me back down again to the car with the guards coming off duty. When I told the story half an hour later at the Spanish checkpoint, they explained that the first petrol station in Spain was thirty kilometres away down towards Jaca. Every inch of the walls of the hut in which this conversation took place was covered in skis and it is the only time in my life that I have seen an 'in earnest' St Bernard dog, complete with brandy flask around its neck. My knowledge of Spanish was stretched to the limit as I struggled to interpret for my travelling companions, a Canadian, a German and an Austrian, all of them skiing enthusiasts and keen to compare notes with the Spanish border guards. I decided I would rather sit in the hut with the St Bernard than explore that savage landscape. Such was my introduction to the legendary wildness and dangers of the Pyrenees.

Some years later, on another trip, I discovered how wrong I had been to be so timid. The journey began unpromisingly enough, with Catalan friends in a car following the snowplough around the tortuous bends of the Toses pass. Their cheerful optimism contrasted with my own nervousness:

'Are you sure that it's safe to go on?'

'Oh yes, no problem.'

'This is nothing.'

'Cheer up, John!'

It was pretty enough but did seem a lot of effort for a day out. But from Toses we descended into another world, the broad, green valley of the Cerdanya. The Cerdanya is a curiosity in many ways, a broad, rather flat valley where you would expect precipitous gorges and canyons. This is the valley of the Segre, a river which actually rises in France, flows almost due west through the Cerdanya and reaches Seu d'Urgell before turning definitively southwards and heading for Lleida and its eventual union with the waters of the Ebre.

The Cerdanya is safe and cosy, even womblike, the rich meadows backed by the impenetrable mountains. It is also an inspirational landscape that raises the spirits of the weary traveller. I think the moment that I fell absurdly, hopelessly and for ever in love with the Cerdanya was as we started the return trip. There was only a little pale winter afternoon light left in the sky, the clouds were gathering heavily over the Cadí range to the south and we were anxious to get at least some way over the pass before night fell completely. The lights were coming on in the sturdy houses with their wooden balconies and shutters and as we drove east along the road, there were the lights of a town, and immediately above it, suspended as it were in the misty sky, the lights of another town. The first was Puigcerdà, the border town. The second was Font Romeu, a winter sports resort across in France. It was a vision of a grander world than the one I thought I knew. Any subsequent attempt to repeat this exquisite moment has ended in failure, and I am now too wise to try. It must have had something to do with the particular weather and lighting conditions that afternoon and perhaps also with that cheerless day enlivened by the good humour of our little party.

With Catalans on both sides of the frontier, there has always been much contact, legal and illegal, between one side and the other, just as happens in the Basque country at the other end of the Pyrenees. Laurie Lee, in *As I Walked Out One Midsummer Morning*, recounts an alarming crossing into Spain in the early months of the Civil War, following his guide in the darkness across the mountain, his only hope of survival keeping up with the shadowy figure hurrying on ahead of him. Cela also tells of an 'unofficial' trip to see a relation on the French side, walking across a remote bit of border in the Vall d'Aran. I did not manage anything as adventurous as either of them, but I did have the quiet satisfaction of crossing the border at least once without any kind of control.

This happened at Llívia, a small Spanish enclave within France, a few miles beyond Puigcerdà. I should perhaps also add a credit for my Editorial Alpina map and guidebook, which has the great advantage for the traveller of treating the Cerdanya as a whole, French and Spanish. Coming back from a visit to the Conflent valley, I reach Sallagosa (Saillagouse) and then, avoiding the international road which carefully skirts the enclave, turned right by the station along the local road through Ro and within five minutes was in Llívia. Llívia manages to exist very much as if Spain and France did not exist. In every place I went into I was asked if I wanted to pay in francs or pesetas. In many ways it is an anachronism, but in other ways it seemed a model of the new Europe in which the making of money can go ahead regardless of history and frontiers and languages, a mini-Andorra. It is a pretty little town with an interesting museum which includes many of the contents of what claims to be the oldest pharmacy in Europe. Across the road, in an old stone tower, is a spectacular exhibition of the flora of the Cerdanya, which shows not only the summer flowers I have seen blooming outside in the meadows but also the brilliant spring flowers, the narcissi and the gentians. The ground floor of this building was used as a prison, but the upper floor was the meeting place of the town council, which was chosen by lot.

Nowadays it is relatively easy to visit the Cerdanya, with a superb new tunnel cutting through the Cadí and a good road (at least good in stretches) straight down the Llobregat valley to Barcelona. Part, at least, of the funding for this new road has come from the European Community as it creates a new through-route from France to Spain. The approach to the tunnel from the south is extremely impressive, with a wide, sweeping road swinging ever closer to the apparently impenetrable rock face. On one unforgettable, clear night a friend of mine turned off the car lights so that we could admire the illusion of snow produced by the moonlight on the white cliffs.

If the tunnel has made it easy to reach the Cerdanya, serious preparation is still required to ascend from the valley to the heights above. One such ascent begins from a fork on the Puigcerdà-Bellver road (which follows the river Segre east-west along the valley) at Ger. From Meranges, which lives from a balanced mixture of farming and tourism, a mountain track climbs wildly upwards through a wilderness of pine forests, wild raspberries and flowers in breathtaking profusion. The intense carmine of the pinks which can be found all over the foothills of the Pyrenees changes to the palest mauve of a frilled variety which dominates the mountain pastures and meadows, the *clavel de pastor* or shepherd's pink. And then there is wild mountain thyme, tiny heathers, several varieties of thistles, camomile and harebells. At the top of this track is the Refugi de Malniu, a mountain refuge which in summer caters for a wider tourist clientele, serving coffee, beer and sandwiches in this cheerful mountain scene.

There is some camping in the rock-strewn meadows, and the air is thin, clear and hot, full of the scent of pines, a dream of suburban English rockeries fulfilled in immense boulders smothered in dwarf junipers and rhododendrons. It is a short but stiff walk from there up to the lake of Malniu. There is a strong sense of country excursions as a shared, communal activity in Catalonia and all the way up there are encouraging comments from people on the path – 'It gets better soon, you'll see,' 'The views up there are wonderful.' Walking up to these high, wild spots is a way of establishing your credentials as a 'good Catalan'. A solitary man of fifty stops to tell me that it's seventeen years since he was last there, and the place is as lovely as ever. But most people are in large family groups, or multi-family groups, chattering cheerfully away with that special sense of being at home – in Catalonia – while being far from home (Barcelona or wherever).

Nearer the lake there is crystal-clear, ice-cold water bubbling from what seem to be a hundred springs beneath our feet. It is intensely ancient, and intensely exciting, this black, silent lake almost surrounded by pine trees, isolated from both the peaks above and the valley below. And that seemingly permanent blue sky above, defying the storm clouds gathering over towards the Cadí and France and Andorra. The trout do not seem to mind the occasional swimmer, though care is needed, for there is only about a foot of sun-warmed water on top of deep, cold Pyrenean mysteries. On the French side, there are hot springs, where nudity is the order of the day (summer and winter!), but in these high, cold tarns both modesty and common sense are required. There are semi-wild horses here too, not the stunted, hairy ponies you might expect, but large, sleek beasts who seem totally unafraid of human beings. Like the sheep and goats and cows, they roam these high pastures with their out-of-tune bells tolling away, making the perfect accompaniment to the flowery wilderness.

Leaving some of the party by the lake, I climbed with my younger children further up the hillside. The lake suddenly disappears and you are in the primaeval landscape at the foot of the Serra Mascarella, climbing to nearly 3,000 metres and the French frontier. It is awesome – as if some enormous rock-crusher had been at work, smashing the ancient rocks to smithereens and flinging them at random across the mountainside. Here by the edge of a bog, marked on the map as another small lake, there is a multicoloured maypole, erected no doubt by one of the *excursionista* groups. Across the short, spongy turf a solitary stallion raises its head, sniffs the air nervously and disappears into a grove of trees. Even at this height, there are still abundant flowers – London Pride, orchids, wild blue delphiniums and a mass of tiny alpine plants I am unable to identify, the dense and ancient vegetation of the wilderness.

The flora of this northern side of the valley, which catches the summer sun and is more inclined to high alpine meadows, is richer and more varied than that in the shadow of the Cadí, which even in summer allows the steep slopes only a few hours of sunshine. They gleam intensely white in the early morning sun, but from mid-morning the shadows lengthen across their slopes, producing by afternoon unforgettable effects of light and shade, especially in those days of late August when this area is especially prone to sudden storms. One of the better walks on this side of the Cerdanya is accessible from a network of mountain tracks that climb up from Martinet on the Bellver to Seu d'Urgell road. There is a parking place at the top of the track and from here a path takes you ever closer to the forbidding mass of the mountain. You become aware not just of the great white limestone cliffs but also the towering banks of grey scree up which the pines march to meet the sheer rock. Like so many walks in the Cerdanya, it ends at a spring with a large grassy depression, probably volcanic, which is a popular picnic spot. Thyme grows abundantly in this part, and beneath the pine trees there are wild raspberries and strawberries and lavender clinging to rocky crevices.

But our picnic is rudely interrupted by angry rumbles of thunder across the valley towards Andorra, and we join what becomes a high-spirited scramble back down the path. This is no country to play with the weather, as the many cracked pines smashed by lightning testify. Fortunately, this storm rumbles on through the afternoon first one way and then the other, and only that night in a prolonged and torrential downpour does it finally reach the valley floor. The mountains are grey and still and sombre. A black eagle hovers over the pine forests, its wings etched against the angry sky, and its high-pitched off-key whistle rising above the low rumble of thunder. As you come to the lower slopes you are conscious of the contrast between the elemental existence above 2,000 metres and the prim, restrained nature of the valley itself, where the characteristic black-and-white cattle graze in the meadow and the hay is being cut and stacked ready for winter feed. We are happy eventually to find safe haven in the crowded paradise of a teashop in Martinet where there is tea and coffee and chocolate, the rich, creamy milk of the Cerdanya, buns and cream cakes and apple tarts and *coca* (a sweet pastry common throughout Catalonia with a variety of nutty, creamy toppings).

If Puigcerdà at the border is the largest town in the Cerdanya, the most attractive on the Spanish side is undoubtedly Bellver. Perhaps it is partly a function of familiarity but Bellver to me has everything that turns the impatient traveller into a romantic dreamer who pauses, sits a while and lets imagination fantasise around the simple reality. At the Font de Talló, a little spring just outside the village, there is a tiny chapel and shrine, a picnic table and wood and stone benches, and on Easter Monday the local children come dressed in national costume to sell sweet wine and *coca* to the locals. The water gurgles gently from the earth, the crickets sing, the wind sighs in the willow trees – the typical sounds of the Cerdanya. And Bellver has a volcano, too, cultivated on the south side where the spring is, but steep and wooded on the side overlooking the village. Its crater is marked by a shallow depression at the top some 6 metres across, with butterflies dancing among the thyme, and the sweet scent of pine permeating the air.

The view from the volcano is especially lovely in winter with the contrast of the still-green meadows of the Cerdanya and the snow-capped tops of the Cadí. There is also an excellent view of the religious buildings at Talló, an Augustinian canonry which predates the village, and still plays an important part in the life of its inhabitants. Village funerals are still held there and the mile or so from village to church is covered on foot along a tree-lined lane. Bellver is a close community and these funeral processions are an important part of village life. The ordered and numbered triangular churchyard is adjacent to the road with some ancient carved stones set into the wall. In summer there are concerts and I was lucky to attend one of these with a large, appreciative, shirt-sleeved audience sitting in the gloomy single nave. We had waited patiently for twenty minutes for the concert to begin. In Barcelona this would be regarded as quite unacceptable, for Barcelona is as punctual as any city in Europe. But in Bellver a cheerful, relaxed optimism prevails among both holiday-makers and villagers. Those who want to live a more frenetic life went off to the city years ago.

Bellver, like most towns and villages in Catalonia, celebrates its *festa major* (main festival) in August. It sums up so well the essence of Bellver as a village that lives in harmony with the natural order of things. On one particular day the main square, an irregular, arcaded space fashioned out of the bare stone at the summit of the little hill on which Bellver sits, was cluttered with stalls selling honey, goat cheeses, cheeses pickled in olive oil and herbs, sausages, dried flowers, and the numerous varieties of mushrooms that are much used in local cuisine. The nicest stalls were those of the local children selling great bunches of herbs and the large yellow ground-hugging thistle; this was used by medieval pharmacists against the plague and can often be seen in winter pinned to doors as a symbol of the sun and rebirth.

'Where did you find the thistles?'

'We went up to the mountains yesterday and got them.'

'They're lovely.'

'We put them on a door, or a gate, or the cow shed. They bring you luck.'

I have one sitting here in my writing shed in the garden on a grey, cheerless, December morning in London.

Goat cheese is a subject which raises much enthusiasm among the Catalans, and is guaranteed to stir the soul of even the most hardened city dweller from Barcelona. I became embroiled in a search for goat cheese that occupied a large part of a hot July afternoon. We found the house where the cheese was made in the village of Bar at the top of another of those rough tracks leading up towards the Cadí from the main road. It has a little church with a slate-capped octagonal tower, a cluster of stone-built farms and cottages with tiled roofs, and spectacular views of the Segre valley below and the Cadí mountains above. We found the house; we also found a magnificent, tethered billy goat, chestnut brown with long curling horns like a curlew's beak, an untethered puppy, which terrorised the most nervous member of our party – who seemed convinced that its puppy enthusiasm was undisguised hostility – and a kitchen full of gleaming and very sophisticated-looking equipment. But despite the best efforts of various local people who directed us further up the mountain where they thought the goat people might be with their flock, we found no-one. There were goat droppings on the path and a distant tolling of bells, which may or may not have been goats. But of anyone prepared to do business with urban Catalans in search of authenticity, nothing. And despite its name, Bar does not even have a local café for thirsty Catalans to refresh themselves in. As the afternoon shadows lengthened into a haze of blues of greens and greys, we bumped happily back down the track again.

The little villages between Bellver and the Cadí tunnel are mellow and friendly and pleasant places to relax in. In the hamlet of Pedra the little Romanesque church seems to grow out of a rocky mound above the houses, the stones gradually becoming more even in the transition from virgin rock to dressed stone wall. The parking place beneath is guarded by a very soft, friendly labrador who attaches herself to my daughters and seems to understand English quite perfectly. At Urus they have reconstructed the old stone wash house by the fountain but it is no longer in use (these communal cold-water wash places are now under serious threat from the spread of electricity and washing machines). A flock of mixed sheep and goats, their bells clanging, are on their way up to the high pastures, which in winter become the skiing slopes of Tossa d'Alp. Their shepherd, in boots and a long-sleeved shirt even though it is high summer, carries his jacket under his arm. Clearly they will be gone for some days. Behind him limps a lame sheepdog, his tail wagging enthusiastically but looking no match for the agile black goats springing on ahead.

Riu, only a couple of hundred metres from the tunnel service area, has a funny little irregular square, sloping quite steeply and almost filled by its church and a children's playground. It is curiously named (in Castilian) the Square of the Constitution of 1921. Coming back in the exquisite evening light, there is a perfect view of Pedra church on its hillock again, with the bare pale heights of Tossa d'Alp above. Bor has a trout farm and a friendly shop-cum-bar and a west porch to its church which is a perfect spot to watch the sun setting through the blue haze of mountains over towards Andorra. There are other curiosities here: a cat-hole in the church door, presumably to help the church cat to hunt its church mice more efficiently; a wooden coffin-bearer attached by cobwebs to the wall, much like those old porters' trolleys which used to adorn disused country stations.

I feel comfortable and safe in the Cerdanya. The flowers of the valley are those that I remember from my childhood in Somerset – poppies, scabious, pink and white dog roses, the delicate, flimsiest stems of the grass, which in Somerset at least is called quaking or even quaker grass. And back in Bellver there are the hours spent over coffee or beer, alone or with friends, in the old-fashioned Café Nou, which the tourists have not yet managed to spoil. It is a busy social centre, sharing an entrance with the cinema, and containing real billiards as well as pool tables, football machines and a television set on which I watched the first half of the 1990 World Cup football England v. Italy third-place match – which should have been the final – with a grumpy, elderly Englishman from Andorra who thought I asked too many questions.

'Why do you live in Andorra?'

'Who do you live with?'

'Where . . .?'

'I've come to watch the football, not to answer your questions!'

He was large, bald, and rather fierce, and I did not argue. In winter I have sat here and kept warm and watched television with a baby daughter now nearly grown-up and then marched out into the cold twilight to hear the music of the sheep and goats returning from the valley meadows to the village, where they will spend the night in the same houses as the farmer and his family, and to buy fresh, warm milk from the dairy. No wonder the French monarchy wanted control over these idyllic fields.

By the treaty of the Pyrenees in 1659, the Catalan counties of Rosselló, Conflent, Vallespir and the upper part of the Cerdanya became part of the French Crown. The keenness of the French to hang on to their new possessions is apparent from the money they spent to employ Vauban and his colleagues to fortify the village of Mont Lluís (Mont Louis) at the head of the Conflent valley and the town of Vilafranca de Conflent (Villefranche-de-Conflent) further down towards Prada (Prades) and Perpinyà (Perpignan). Mont Lluís was a new fortress controlling the entrance to the Conflent valley from the Cerdanya, but Vilafranca had been fortified since the early Middle Ages. It was seized by the French in 1654 and, fearing that if the Catalans took it back again the French forces in the Cerdanya would be cut off, they moved swiftly to demolish most of the medieval fortifications. But in the years of uneasy peace and intermittent war which followed 1659, the fortifications of the town were rebuilt by Vauban. The results are a striking mixture of the advanced ideas of Vauban and remnants of an earlier age, the contrast being most apparent at the 'French' end where the old and new 'Gates of France' overlook the junction of the Tet and Cady rivers.

Nowadays, Vilafranca is much more uniformly a tourist event than anything on the Spanish side, its narrow streets, where the streams flow winter and summer, packed with restaurants and craft shops full of wool, leather, dried flowers, honey and jam, herbs and spices. People seem quicker and busier here. There are 'We speak Catalan' signs in shops and even 'We are Catalan' slogans by the roadside. But the Catalan names of villages are posted below the French names, and the Catalan effort seems less natural this side of the border. One is led to the suspicion that the French may have been much more effective than the Spanish in eliminating the indigenous language and culture, much as the English did in the Scottish Highlands a century later after the 1745 uprising. Only the verger at Vilafranca church seemed keen to talk Catalan to me. And he was very ancient indeed:

'You live here, in the village?'

'No, in Perpinyà. I come up to help for two months every summer.'

Catalan language and culture seem to be on the defensive in what the nationalists call Catalunya Nord (North Catalonia), rather confirming some impressions I had gathered that summer before entering Spain. There are superficial signs of a Catalan consciousness in Rousillon. The motorway south from Narbonne has been christened 'La Catalane', but the road signs are strictly in French. The last service area before Spain advertises a Village Catalane, but it is immediately obvious that Catalanism on this side of the border is merely a way of selling a little local colour to the tourists. The woman in the tourist office admitted to me that there was no local government structure which reflected the historical existence of Catalonia and no official recognition of the language:

'What, none at all?'

'Well, some villages are difficult, and insist on having their village signs in Catalan as well as French.'

But she reserved her greatest scorn for visitors from the other side of the Pyrenees:

'They come over on visits and insist on speaking to everyone in Catalan. It's ridiculous. This is France!'

This conversation took place against an enormous blow-up of a photograph of the *sardana* being danced in the heart of Perpinyà.

One town on the French side that still plays an important role in Catalan cultural life is Prada, the home for many years of Pau Casals. But its music festival has declined considerably in importance since his death, and the only Catalan reference I could find in the 1990 programme was to the Catalan pianist, Maria de la Pau. But the Catalan Summer University at Prada continues to thrive, and is now in its twenty-second season. Begun in response to the university upheavals of 1968, it is an important forum for free and open intellectual debate (in Catalan) of not just the issues of direct relevance to cultural nationalism, but also the most pressing issues of the times. So 1990 devoted major attention to developments in Eastern Europe, and also to ecological issues.

While the motorway crossing from France into Spain is probably very boring compared with, say, Laurie Lee's trek across the mountains under the cover of darkness, or the tragic, pitiful, final retreat of the republicans in 1939, it still raises some interesting issues. If the Village Catalane is a monument to consumerism, the symbolism of the Porta Catalana (Catalan Gate) back on the Spanish side is very different. Its uncompromising concrete modernity, with the flag of Catalonia prominently carved above the motorway, is a clear statement about both national identity and the belief in progress. This is one of the last works of the Catalan architect Josep-Lluís Sert and must be one of the few motorway service stations in the world which could be called architecture. Straddling the motorway like a Roman triumphal arch, it begs the question of whether this is the 'gateway to Catalonia' (i.e., the four Spanish provinces that make up the Generalitat) or an 'archway within Catalonia' (i.e., a broader definition of the Catalan lands, including those north of the Pyrenees). Either interpretation is possible.

Chapter 8

Barcelona: Progress, Problems and Possibilities

From about 1850, strange buildings started appearing on the coast of Catalonia; buildings that reflected not just the wealth of their owners, but new and exotic tastes in design; houses that flaunted ostentatiously the wealth of their owners in complicated structures of stone, glass, ceramics and metal, with motifs of exotic fruits and animals and birds. These were the houses of the *indianos* or *americanos*, Catalans who had made their fortunes in America, especially in Cuba and Puerto Rico, which remained Spanish colonies until 1898, and had come home to exhibit and invest their wealth. Not only private houses were built: there was also an explosion of monuments and mausoleums in cemeteries and of public fountains and schools donated by the returning emigrants. This explains why, for example, the small industrial and fishing town of Vilanova i La Geltrú has a railway station that looks more like a colonial palace.

The big Catalan revival had begun in the mid-eighteenth century. At one level it was a bad moment for Catalans, their institutions suppressed by the Bourbon kings, their language reduced to a spoken language only. But the Bourbons in Spain had advanced ideas on economics, and the Catalans benefited most from the liberalisation of trade with America, and the ending of Seville's monopoly. During the second half of the century, the increasingly confident bourgeoisie established a number of bodies in Barcelona, such as the Chamber of Commerce, which helped to forge their identity as the new leaders of Catalan society. For the rest of Spain, economic modernisation foundered in the years of the Napoleonic Wars and the collapse of the American empire. But for Barcelona it was the beginning of economic growth which continued almost without interruption up to the outbreak of the Civil War in 1936.

By 1800, Barcelona was a town of nearly 100,000 people, still tightly constrained by the city walls. Barcelona shared the narrow plain between the mountains and the sea with a group of little villages – Sants, Les Corts, Sarrià, Sant Gervasi, Horta, Gràcia, Clot – all names preserved in the suburbs of the modern city. But of all the settlements outside the walls, only the Barceloneta, the fishing district where the city's best fish restaurants are still to be found, was an integral part of the city. It had been built to replace the district destroyed by the Bourbons in 1714 to build their fortress – the Cuitadella – which in turn became the site of the 1888 Universal Exhibition, and is now shared by such incongruous activities as the zoo, the modern art museum and the Catalan parliament, all in a park setting.

Through the century, the population rose steadily, reaching 184,000 by 1857, 337,000 in 1877 and 500,000 by the end of the century. There was steady movement into Barcelona from the rural areas, and a transformation of society from a traditional rural peasantry ruled by a landed aristocracy to an urban proletariat controlled by an industrial and commercial bourgeoisie. Already by 1850, more than a quarter of the population of Catalonia lived in Barcelona. This was in marked contrast to the rest of Spain, where life went on much as before, deeply rooted in the problems and perspectives of the past.

It is against this backdrop of dynamic social and economic change that one of the most radical and comprehensive town-planning exercises of nineteenth-century Europe was drawn up, the results of which still reverberate through the city today. This was the Cerdà Plan, an ambitious project to extend the city beyond the confines of the old city walls. The Eixample (Extension), as it came to be called, was designed as a grid pattern, with blocks measuring 133 metres each way, and cut through by two parallel, diagonal avenues – the Paral·lel, from Plaça de Espanya to the port, where much of the city's old-fashioned theatre and nightlife is concentrated, and the Diagonal, now extended out into the university city. The other main axis is the Gran Vía, three times wider than the average street, running roughly parallel to the sea just north of the Plaça de Catalunya and ending in the Plaça de Espanya at the foot of Montjuïc.

Cerdà was a man of progressive ideas. Not least, he wanted to unite working class and bourgeoisie, town and country. The plan was designed so that the rigid geometry of the grid would be softened by parks and gardens, allowing only two sides of each grid square to be built upon. But this proved utopian in practice. The pressure of soaring property values and a rampant provincial bourgeoisie meant that almost all available land was built on. Green spaces and the working class were equally excluded. General knowledge of exactly how the Eixample came to be developed has greatly increased thanks to the exhibition lodged in Gaudí's Casa Milà (popularly known as La Pedrera – the quarry) for much of 1990. This exhibition had the great advantage of singling out 150 buildings in the Eixample for particular attention, all identified by their *Quadrat d'Or* (golden square) banners. It was followed by a large exhibition and associated publishing on *Modernisme* (Catalan art nouveau).

What had been intended as an expansive development became, under the pressure of speculative building, a very dense development dominated by increasingly high-rise blocks of flats. Property became a crucial way of investing fortunes made in Cuba or Puerto Rico or the textile industry. Architecture was used in a way that is very familiar to us today, as a selling point. It is an architecture of façades, a statement of prestige. This is especially obvious in the Rambla de Catalunya (not to be confused with the old-town *rambla*) and the Passeig de Gràcia, always the two most prestigious streets of the Eixample. But it was also an architecture of a confident middle class with international pretensions. The design net was cast very wide indeed, and from about 1870, classicism was replaced by eclecticism as the driving principle of design.

It should also be understood that what the visitor sees today is in some ways a rather arbitrary collection of buildings. Many of those built between 1860 and 1900 were torn down to make way for bigger, taller blocks, and especially in the years 1900–15 there was constant rebuilding in the Passeig de Gràcia. There was also the desire to improve existing buildings, and *Modernisme*, as an architecture of façades, was well placed to take on this role too. In addition, improvements in local transport dictated a progressive movement upward and outward of wealthy people, often turning summer villas in the surrounding villages into permanent homes. By 1913, Sarrià was a busy, thriving community with first-class coaches and basket armchairs on the local train.

Most of the architectural tendencies which flourished in Europe either side of the year 1900 can be found in the busy streets of the Eixample, as the local architects and builders felt their way towards the style which was eventually to gain international recognition as *Modernisme*. For while Cerdà's plan shows an ambivalence between the rational classicism of the plan and the Romantic utopianism which was later to be called the Garden City, the outpourings of Catalan architecture fit clearly within a Romantic historicist framework of neo-Gothic, neo-Arab, neo-Romanesque. Yet just as the *Renaixença* (the Catalan cultural rebirth) was rediscovering national cultural and political identity, so there is a clear consensus towards emphasising those forms (Romanesque and Gothic) and those materials (wrought iron, tile) which connected with a dream of Catalonia's great past.

Visitors will find much to admire in almost any block of the central part of the Eixample, but it is probably best to start at the block commonly known as the Mançana de la Discòrdia (Block of Discord) because of the contrasting styles of its three best-known buildings. Located immediately outside the Passeig de Gràcia railway station, it is the perfect introduction to the idiosyncrasies of Barcelona. For many people it is also their introduction to Antoni Gaudí, architect and national symbol. Born at Reus in 1852, he emerged from the confusion of styles in late nineteenth-century Barcelona as the most individual architect of his generation. He enjoyed the patronage of the rich industrialist Eusebi Güell. A deeply religious man, the project to build a new cathedral (the Sagrada Familia, or Holy Family) occupied him almost exclusively in the later years of his life right up to his death in 1926.

Gaudí's Casa Batlló of 1904–6 has a polychromatic, tiled façade, balconies moulded like primitive masks and irregular flowing window openings on the ground and first floor. The roof, always an excuse for Gaudí to indulge his more fantastic and humorous imagination, is like an illustration of Hansel and Gretel's gingerbread house in its use of colour and fantastic motifs. What distinguishes this building is that it is an integral design, from façade to fittings and furniture, with elaborate work in ceramic tiles, metalwork, wood and stained glass.

Immediately next door, and the earliest of the three key buildings, is the Casa Amatller of Josep Puig i Cadalfach. The success of this building is that it gives the illusion of being a small Gothic palace rather than the block of flats it has always been. There is splendid Gothic tracery and carving on the lower floors, and a more fanciful tiled, stepped gable on top which gives the illusion of an Arabian palace crossed with a Dutch town house from Delft or Alkmaar. The Gothic is in any case strictly eclectic, including, for example, carvings of monkeys round the windows which are a reference to the client's status as a cocoa merchant! Puig i Cadalfach is also a name that is important in Catalan politics, as a leading member of the big business party of Prat de la Riba – the Lliga Catalana, and thus makes explicit the links between historicism in art and architecture and romantic nationalism in politics. Incredibly, he was not allowed to practise as an architect after the Civil War and lived mainly in French Catalonia, working on his researches into Romanesque art.

The third building is the corner block known as the Casa Lleó Morera by Lluís Domènech i Montaner. Only a few years ago I described it as being 'badly mutilated', but since then it has undergone extensive repairs which have returned it to something like the graceful elegance of its original state. If the external stonework is impressive enough but rather austere, the interior is visually very exciting. There is a small patio and staircase rather like those to be found in the medieval town houses of Montcada Street. This is an arts and crafts paradise, with stained glass, metal lamp fixtures, wood and stone carving. There is an emphasis on the domestic with carvings of pet animals. Above the staircase soars a glass roof in pink and mauve and yellow. Mosaic murals depict the life of the family who owned the house (the usual convention was for the family to occupy the first floor, which is thus both externally and internally the most interesting in design terms), and there are mosaic floors and stained glass windows too. And all of this is now open to visitors, for the first floor is occupied by the offices of the Barcelona tourist board.

These buildings of the Passeig de Gràcia are at their best on a winter morning when the oblique sunlight shows off the delicate tones of stone, ceramics and glass to full advantage. Those who are prepared to tolerate the noise and exhaust fumes which disfigure this magnificent avenue can sit for a while on the benches beneath the wrought-iron lamp-standards and dream themselves back to the heroic days of the Catalan bourgeoisie, when money bought not only the recognised and the conventional, but also the esoteric, the nostalgic and the outright perverse. It is easy to imagine them parading up and down this great avenue in their fine clothes, flaunting their wealth to their neighbours, or in their boxes at the Liceu Opera House, taking more interest in the latest fashion and gossip than in the latest opera by Wagner or Verdi.

If Puig i Cadalfach represents the conservative strand of Catalan nationalism, Domèmech i Montaner stands for a more populist politics. This is reflected in his other two prizewinning buildings, the Palace of Catalan Music (1908) and Hospital de Sant Pau (1912). The Palau is, of all the modernist buildings in Barcelona, the most accessible and the most nearly perfect. Yet it has been dramatically modified in recent years to update the facilities for both performers and audience. This has involved opening up the ground floor on one side, and putting in a new glass and steel wall to create both extra space and an external staircase that rises the full height of the three-storey building. This has also enabled a modern box office to be constructed at the far end and a new headquarters for the Orfeó Català choir, dominated by a round brick tower growing like a palm tree from a rough, moulded root. This extension includes archives, a library and a music school. In the centre of the ground floor, the only part of the interior open to visitors as opposed to concert-goers, a wood and glass *modernista* bar has been constructed.

The success of the Palau depends to a great extent on its rationalism – the way that the steel frame creates a framework for the glass and other applied arts in which the building is so rich. Its great centrepiece is the central stained glass boss in the ceiling, with its repeated motif of a pre-Raphaelite head with flowing auburn hair. The colours modulate and deepen from blue and green and mauve on the edges of the ceiling to yellow and gold at the base of the boss. On each side are four great crowns of lights, set at an angle of some thirty degrees to the horizontal, made of coloured glass and metal and ceramic diamonds. The orchestra is backed by a ceramic frieze of the muses of music, young women carrying musical instruments linked by garlands, their upper parts sculpted in high relief, their lower parts flat and elongated. The garland motif is picked up in the windows of both the circle and upper circle, interspersed with the flags of Catalonia and of Saint George.

In contrast to these light, airy motifs is the Gothic weight of the stone Walkyries (above a bust of Beethoven) which reflect the great enthusiasm for Wagner in Barcelona at the turn of the century. German Romanticism was an exotic, exciting world of strange passions and titanic struggles, but the Catalans could also look back with pride to a past when they had also been a great and proud nation. On the other side of the proscenium arch is a great stone tree and the bust of Anselm Clavé, to whom Catalan musical life, and especially the choral tradition, owes so much. David Mackay, an English architect living and working in Barcelona, has written in his book on *modernista* architecture (first published in English by The Anglo-Catalan Society) that the Palau expresses in architecture the universality of music, which in turn reflects the ambitions of the Catalan bourgeoisie for international recognition. It must be added that not all travellers share my view of the Palau. John Langdon-Davies, in *Gatherings from Catalonia*, called the Palau 'the worst and most inappropriately conceived concert hall in the world'. Barcelona's new international concert hall, jointly financed by the Generalitat and town hall, no doubt has better acoustics and facilities, but possibly not the emotional appeal of the Palau.

Domènech i Montaner's second great socially committed work is the Hospital de Sant Pau. Here the architect insisted on developing the building as a system of linked pavilions across no less than four blocks of the Eixample. He took advantage of the sloping site to set the buildings at an angle of forty-five degrees to the gridiron. This angle is continued in a short diagonal road, now pedestrianised, which leads down to Gaudí's Sagrada Familia cathedral. George Orwell wished the anarchists had destroyed it in 1936. I have never found anything good to say about the Sagrada Familia and prefer to write about the Gaudí buildings I do like. It is still a source of controversy in Barcelona, and in July 1990 this even reached the ears of BBC Radio Four listeners, who were treated to an account of a 'cultural demonstration' outside the cathedral in opposition to the grotesque sculptural figures of the crucifixion by Josep Maria Subirachs recently placed on the façade of the passion. One hundred people, the great majority of them opposed to the sculptures, climbed up onto an improvised platform to vilify the sculptor over the loudspeakers. The dramatic high point of the evening was a Japanese woman making a passionate speech in Japanese from the rostrum. Nobody understood, but everybody applauded. Such is the passion that this unfinished building still arouses.

For me, then, the Sagrada Familia is merely a point of departure for the walk along to the Hospital. At the halfway point, Gaudí's towers already look heavy and contrived in comparison with the airy Gothic pinnacle on the Hospital façade. It is surrounded by a wrought-iron fence on brick and ceramic plinths, and through the main entrance there is an enticing view of the gardens in which the other pavilions are set. Domènech's technical achievement here was to bury underground the many piped services required in a hospital. He was then able to create, behind the imposing entrance building, a kind of garden suburb, with each department occupying a single-storey building with easy access to fresh air, sunshine and flowers. Much use is made of ceramic tile decoration throughout, and the whole effect is the opposite of the massive institutionalised architecture that often seems to be the fate of modern hospitals.

For Oriol Bohigas, the distinguished architect and writer on architecture and urbanism who is one third of the Martorell, Bohigas and Mackay partnership, Domènech represents the rational side of *Modernisme* while Gaudí sums up its expressive side. Certainly there is nothing in Domènech's work which in any way compares to La Pedrera, Gaudí's curvilinear corner block in the Passeig de Gràcia. The back is as interesting as the front, with curving walls and iron balconies alive with flowerpots and washing lines. The interior space of this particular block is a pleasant jumble of gardens and small buildings. There are now guided tours of the roof. On the particular evening that I visited the roof, there were two guides, and in a rare gesture of solidarity, the Catalans agreed to join with the Spanish so that there could also be a tour in English! It was on the roof where Gaudí, as at the Casa Batlló, hoped to let his imagination run riot. The year was 1912 and he was laid off before the building was completed, so only some of the chimneys are decorated with tiles and anthropomorphic sculptural effects in the way Gaudí had wished. It was to be his last civil building. For the rest of his life Gaudí concentrated on religious buildings – the crypt of the church at the Colònia Güell, completed in 1916, and the Sagrada Familia, of which only the façade of the nativity had been completed at his death in 1926. He is an architect of contradictions, a rationalist builder in the neo-Gothic tradition who loved extravagant, expressionist designs, and a conservative Catholic devoted to radical new directions in architecture.

The Milà family, who had commissioned La Pedrera, disliked the finishes intensely. This was particularly unfortunate as it was only the first floor, intended for their occupation, which had a complete Gaudí decor. They removed the broken-tile decoration from the bathrooms and kitchen, and in later years had the whole flat redecorated in French classical style. Now it has been rehabilitated as an open-plan exhibition area, and this emphasises the great freedom of space Gaudí was able to use in this building as opposed to the 'mere façades' of so many of the Eixample blocks. He used a steel web and slanting columns of brick and stone to give complete freedom of layout on each floor, but always with an emphasis on flowing, curvilinear forms. The ceilings of the first floor, finished in undulating plaster, are of startling originality. The prospects for this building are excellent as it was bought in 1986 by the Caixa de Catalunya Savings Bank, who are restoring it as the head office of their cultural foundation.

It is not my intention simply to list all the Gaudí buildings in Barcelona – the local tourist office will be delighted to provide such information. But I do want to mention two more places which have always given me intense personal pleasure. Firstly the Güell Park. This has ended up as a park in the English sense of the word, but was originally laid out as a garden suburb on the hills above the town for the rich and aristocratic industrialist Count Eusebi Güell. What was built, the two pavilions at the entrance, the staircase with the lizard (or, maybe, dragon) fountain, the great open terrace with its curving retaining wall decorated with all manner of broken pots and tiles and the forest-like undercroft intended as the marketplace of the development, are works of genius, by which I mean individual and original designs linked to complete control of the technical means.

The Güell Park is a place for children and those who love children. Children are enchanted by the colour and playfulness of the design, and by the semi-wild areas of pines and shrubs further up the hill with their distant views of the city and the sea and closer views of ceramic-encrusted towers. There is a word of warning here for the visitor. It has always been difficult to reach the Güell Park. The N° 100 tourist bus goes there but will drop you at an entrance above the park. To get the full impact you need to walk not down but up into the park through Gaudí's own entrance, which is like a subtle course of psychotherapy designed to bring out the child in each of us. So the best course is either to walk up from the Plaça Lesseps or be very firm with a taxi driver about where you want to be dropped. Whichever way you come, if it is summer there will be a gentle breeze to welcome you, ice cream to cool you and beer to quench your thirst!

The other Gaudí trip involves a railway journey from the Plaça de Espanya station on the line that heads up the Llobregat valley towards Montserrat. I have two memories of the Colònia Güell – one concerns broad beans and the other Japanese tourists. The word *colònia* in Catalan suggests a workers' village, rather on the lines of Port Sunlight or Bournville. There are a number of precedents, especially in the valley of the upper Llobregat, where mill owners were accustomed to build houses for their workers around the factory. Each of these settlements is dominated by the twin peaks of the church and the owner's house, usually in places of some eminence. But the Güell settlement was built on much more progressive lines, with the school occupying a domi-nant position at one end of the village and the church hiding away in a pine wood at the other.

The settlement is surrounded by the fertile fields of the Llobre-gat valley, which is where the broad beans were growing strongly on a sunny winter's day in the late 1960s. Since then, Gaudí's status has grown considerably and internationally, which is where the Japanese tourists of the late 1980s come in. David Mackay goes so far as to compare it to Le Corbusier's pilgrim chapel at Ronchamp as an innovatory piece of church architec-ture, and I was delighted to find that he shared my long-held view that it was Gaudí's best single building. What one visits is, of course, only the crypt, and it is perhaps fortunate that the church itself was never constructed. Undoubtedly it would have detracted from the crypt with its highly original walls like concertinaed pieces of paper standing on end. We all know this is the best way to stand a piece of paper up, and the architect adapted this simple, rational principle to his building. The glass, the fittings, even the furniture have all miraculously survived changing tastes and tumultuous events. It is what the Sagrada Familia can never be – a place of pilgrimage.

The dictatorship of Primo de Rivera (1923–31) marked a hiatus in modern Catalan history, and in architecture too. The 1920s were the years of the building of the palace on Montjuïc and the other buildings associated with the exhibition of 1929. And also the years of that motley collection of buildings known as the Spanish Village, also on Montjuïc. This has always been an embarrassment to the Catalans, and for years has been in a rather dilapidated, not to say tatty, state. Yet it is still a major attraction to foreign tourists, and I feel that if the Catalans could bite the bullet and accept it as a statement about the rest of Spain, rather than as some kind of attempt at cultural assassination of Catalonia, they might well find the funds to restore it. The contrast between the decadence of Catalan architecture and what was going on in the rest of the world is best demonstrated by that icon of modern architecture, Mies van der Rohe's German pavilion from the 1929 exhibition, now happily rebuilt a stone's throw from both National Palace and Spanish Village.

Whatever arguments there may be about the exact relationship between art and politics, there is no doubt that architecture and politics are inextricably linked. For architecture embodies in itself our views of what the good life is, and who should enjoy it. It expresses, too, the balance or lack of it between individual and social goods, and between the comforts of the body and the aspirations of the soul. So it was in the 1930s. Under the Republic and the Generalitat, Barcelona saw a brief but intense flowering of social architecture, in particular the work of Josep Maria Sert and his associates. This was the Catalan arm (GATCPAC) of the international modern style as espoused by CIAM (International Congress of Modern Architecture) and their committee (CIRPAC). In Catalan art, their ideas were reflected in the work of the ADLAN group, the 'friends of the new art'. In 1970 a commemorative exhibition was opened at the College of Architects in Barcelona, and I was lucky enough to visit it before 'the authorities' closed it down. Again, the political links were clear: the windows of the ground floor of the building were painted in the colours of the Spanish Republic.

It was in the same College of Architects on Saint George's Day 1990 that I met David Mackay, a modest Englishman full of youthful enthusiasm for his chosen career of architecture. Born in Eastbourne, he married a Catalan woman and has lived in Barcelona since 1959. Since 1961 he has been in partnership with Josep Martorell and Oriol Bohigas in a firm that is becoming world-famous for its public architecture. MacKay told me that not only Sert's continuing personal contact with young Catalan architects, but the presence of his buildings in Barcelona, had been an important influence. He drew my attention particularly to a building I had discovered only a few days before, just a few yards from the old university where I had worked for two whole years. But in those days, neither modern architecture nor Sert were subjects of daily conversation. Sert's Dispensari Antitubercolós (TB clinic) of 1934–8 is not only an important milestone in international architecture in its formal simplicity, it also has important local references. For Sert the local was of equal importance to the modern: 'In my architecture the presence of the Mediterranean element is fundamental, a nostalgia for climate and light, of all those visual contacts received in the years of youth in the country where I was born.'

The entrance is through a patio contained within the arm of the L-shaped building, the consulting rooms are placed on the shaded side of the buildings and corridors on the sunny side to resist the summer heat, and great use is made of green tiles in the exterior cladding as well as the more international reference of glass tiles. The most remarkable fact of all is that, with all the other demands on the Republic's limited resources in the middle of a bitter civil war, the clinic was completed. It deserves to be better known and stands as a fitting monument to the humanitarian aims of Spanish and Catalan republicanism.

There were also considerable advances in the design and construction of blocks of flats, noticeably the Casa Bloc in the suburb of Sant Andreu. This estate, with its central park and community buildings, but preserving the urban aspect of the street front, sank into even deeper obscurity than the TB clinic, and only in recent years has it been rediscovered. As Mackay put it: 'It is a milestone in architecture but nobody knew about it because of the Civil War and the Second World War. And therefore it never got into the history books, no-one realised it was built.' He saw it as an example of 'how enormously progressive architecture was here – and it always is, because it takes what's going on around the world and then mellows it immediately to fit into the Barcelona context'.

Mackay's own development in the Barceloneta, the traditional fishing district of Barcelona, is in a way a tribute to the GATCPAC architects in general and the Casa Bloc in particular. It occupies the site of an old engineering factory and the monumental archway entrance has been cleaned and restored. There is the same idea of the quiet interior area as a shared but private space, with little bow windows on the ground floor, and the buildings preserving the line and life of the street. Thus on one side there is an arcade with a pleasant little café where I sat on a hot July morning, drinking beer, crunching hard, dry cheese and chatting to the barman.

'Do you get a lot of visitors to see these houses?'

'Oh yes, only yesterday a French architect came to take pictures.'

'And do people like living here?'

He seemed remarkably well informed: 'Oh yes, these duplex flats are a different aesthetic. In Barcelona people live in flats, everything on the same level. Here they can be like the Americans and go upstairs to bed.'

Opposite the café are the more standard Barceloneta blocks of flats with washing out to dry on the balconies, green shutters, iron bars at the ground-floor windows, peeling paint and chipped rendering, a goldfinch in a cage. Moments later the only other man sitting at the bar crosses the road and takes the hot and agitated goldfinch back inside the cool dark house.

But this is to anticipate slightly. From 1950 onwards, Barcelona, still recovering from the impact of its own war and the World War, deprived of Marshall Aid, became the focus of massive immigration from other parts of Spain. These new Catalans had their characteristic form of architecture too – the shanty town, while at the other end of the social scale the 'victors' of the war were building flats and houses in their own image in the select new suburbs above the city. Although a start was made on social housing in the late 1950s, it was always of a poor quality, with little investment in the infrastructure of the city – roads, lighting, schools, hospitals. And as fast as one shanty town was knocked down, another would spring up. To understand what Barcelona was like in the 1950s and 1960s it is necessary to go to the cities of the South (the so-called Third World), to Calcutta or Managua or Soweto. In Catalonia something of this social drama can still be sensed in the coastal textile town of Mataró, where there are still a few shanties on the hillsides cheek-by-jowl with fortified villas and savage guard dogs of the fortunate few.

One result of this was that architects like Mackay and his partners were drawn not just into thinking about how to build better houses, but how to build a better city, and the political conditions under which this might happen. At a popular level, pressure was brought to bear, too, by the neighbourhood associations, which were very important in the last years of the dictatorship and the transition to democracy (1975 onwards).

Seen as non-political, but with many communist members, they proved an important pressure group for the civilising of Barcelona and of other large Catalan towns. They explain, too, the continuing importance of communists in Catalan local government, where they are seen not only as people who care, but also as people who get things done. Oriol Bohigas has been particularly active in writing about this new vision of the city, and one of his books is called significantly *The Reconstruction of Barcelona*. As David Mackay put it, 'We've always been concerned about urban design.' He argued to me that modern cities need some sense of an 'author', who can draw together the contributions of planners, architects, traffic engineers and so on. 'The individual architect or the individual building can't make a city' seemed to me to sum up his approach.

In the suburbs of Barcelona, it requires a leap of the imagination to understand the contrast between the new attempt to 'urbanise' the city and the wastelands that went before. Barcelona has turned its back on urban motorways and developed instead, from the Eixample with its broad long streets, the idea of the street as not only a way through a particular part of the city, but also a unifying force. There is no attempt to sanitise the city by separating pedestrians and traffic, apart of course from the old medieval nucleus of the city where the streets are too narrow in any case to tolerate motorised transport.

There has been a particular attempt to revitalise open public spaces, which are seen as an essential part of the life style and indeed a symbol of the kind of open, democratic, participatory society that the Barcelona authorities want to build. This was exemplified for me by a local radio show I picked up on my car radio one day while driving out through the hot, dusty, crowded city towards the coast and the beaches. Local councillors are invited to appear and to answer questions about the district they represent, questions covering the urban fundamentals of street lighting, car parking, community facilities, future building plans and so on. First names were the order of the day and callers spoke in Catalan or Castilian, whichever came easier. The councillor, Rosa, was invited to visit particular streets to see problems for herself, or to come to a party to meet local people and celebrate their successes. It seemed to me a good example of what Oriol Bohigas has called 'urbanism that begins with the problems rather than the solutions'.

This same district, Nou Barris, has acquired in the Plaça Lluchmajor a remarkable monument as part of its own urbanisation. This is the monument to the First Spanish Republic, also called the monument to Pi i Margall after its first (and Catalan) president. So now the square is dominated by a tall steel needle at the foot of which is Josep Viladomat's *noucentista* statue of a woman. She represents both the spirit of the Mediterranean and the life-giving qualities of republicanism. Originally, the statue had been placed at the junction of the Passeig de Gràcia and the Diagonal in 1934, but was removed by the Franquists in 1939 and only resurfaced years later in a municipal warehouse. In the new, monarchist Spain, it was considered inappropriate to replace it in the city centre, and it has thus found a new home in Nou Barris. And so it goes . . . Open spaces, squares, places where people can both pass through and linger, statues and monuments, these are the stuff of Barcelona's *nou urbanisme*.

The radio programme I referred to was called the '1993 Show' and this brings me on to the culmination of the reconstruction of Barcelona – the 1992 Olympic Games. The reader who has followed the general line of argument that runs through this book will not be surprised to discover that even 'Olympic Barcelona' has its history. The main stadium on Montjuïc will probably be the oldest stadium ever to house an Olympic Games. The idea of a stadium on Montjuïc dates back to the early 1920s and the failed attempt to secure the nomination of Barcelona for the 1924 Olympics. It was inaugurated in 1929 as part of the development of Montjuïc in connection with the 1929 exhibition, in a style resonant of the spirit of the times, the classical Mediterranean atmosphere of *Noucentisme*. In 1936 the stadium was the chosen venue for the People's Olympiad, an attempt to set up an alternative to the Berlin Games which were due to be held in Hitler's Germany. This boycott was supported by the Popular Front governments in both France and Spain. But the proposal was overtaken by the outbreak of the Spanish Civil War in July 1936 and the field left clear for Hitler and Jesse Owens. 5,000 athletes had registered for Barcelona 1936, and 200 of them stayed on to become the first volunteers of the Republican International Brigades.

There are four Olympic sites. The main stadium is part of a large complex at Montjuïc called the Olympic Ring. In essence this creates a visual link between the various buildings, old and new, where the main events of the Games are to be held, located on three broad terraces. The Ring is thus a sweeping, dipping, concrete curve beginning at the level of the stadium and ending far below it. While I like the overall design, the individual buildings are as yet unconvincing. Even the Sant Jordi sports hall, by the Japanese architect Arata Isozaki, whatever its merit as a highly flexible, high-tech indoor sports arena, seems tainted externally by a rather vulgar and decayed classicism. Ricard Bofill's Sports University is a conscious, and all-too-successful attempt to reflect the *Noucentisme* of the 1929 buildings.

I made the effort to visit the Vall d'Hebron site on one of those still leaden July days which makes one doubt the wisdom of holding the Olympics in Barcelona at all. The city lay shrouded in dense smog beneath me, and every yard along the road from the Montgou tube station was a struggle. Finding the way was a problem in itself.

'The velodrome?'

'I don't know. Ask someone else.'

'The velodrome?'

'That way.' (I was going in the opposite direction.) 'You see the two metal globes on the hillside? It's over that way.'

I hoped they were water tanks but they looked like a miniature atomic reactor. The sun, and here I am remembering a passage in Laurie Lee, was an unwelcome travelling companion, glued to my every step. Trees and grass appeared as I approached the velodrome which I had come to see. And there on the grass lay the crumpled concrete of Joan Brossa's poem, which consists mainly of bits and pieces of punctuation marks; it seemed to me to represent a writer's nightmare, the ultimate writer's block. It was my last day in the city and I was longing for the mountains and the beach! I must say, though, that the velodrome was eventually well worth it. Built in 1984, it has a wonderful sense of speed and dynamism, an apotheosis of Italian futurism. It is all curves and angles and excitement, the antithesis of the gawky solidity of the Olympic Stadium or the smooth lines of Wembley Stadium. Chuck Berry had been playing there the night before. It was a good sign.

Behind the velodrome is the park of the Labyrinth, where, for some reason, water, which was in short supply in the rest of the city, was in abundance. Sprinklers played on green lawns and water ran along little canals and dripped from mossy fountains.

Exotic flowers bloomed in the deep shade of palms, holm oaks and pines. The air was filled with the shrieks of frogs and crickets, birdsong and the excited laughter of children picnicking in a deep, cool secret place that may once have been a quarry. Other children were busy in the maze itself, made from profligate evergreens, observed by anxious adults on an elevated balustrade with two little Roman temples. It was good to escape from the Olympic Games for an hour.

The most exciting part of the preparations for the Olympics for somebody as deeply ambivalent about organised sport as I am is the Olympic Village, in which the Martorell, Bohigas and Mackay partnership is heavily involved. It is the best example of what David Mackay meant when he explained to me how Barcelona was using the Olympics to catch up with the rest of Europe, but learning from the errors of other cities. He saw Barcelona 'on the brink of being one of the major European cities and offering all the best facilities on the same level as other cities do at the moment but with a certain sparkle that they won't have'. It is a sparkle that is not just there in the new buildings going up all over Barcelona, but is reflected in the stylish Catalan approach to everything, from the cut of a shirt to the decor of a bar or the lively conversations that fill the streets of Barcelona at every hour of day and night.

Barcelona owes its importance to its port and yet has been cut off from the sea by railways and docks and factories. But the movement of the main focus of the port to the south of Montjuïc has left a large area for redevelopment. The urban design for this by MBM will include the housing of the Olympic Village. But this is not seen as an end in itself: 'We actually designed it not for the '92 Olympics but for 1993. It's been designed as the city reaching the sea.' For the first time, Mackay explained, the athletes would be housed in a 'real city rather than a suburban development'. The redevelopment of the five kilometres from Montjuïc to the Besós river will include new beaches, restaurants, a sporting port which he hopes will become '*the* European base for nautical activities, and right in the heart of Barcelona'. The refashioning of the old Passeig de Colom fronting the harbour, already referred to, is an integral part of this process of reopening Barcelona to the sea, as is the renovation of the maritime museum in the Drassanes and the project to revive many of the old customs and traditions relating to the sea.

Barcelona in 1993 looks like being a great city to be in. In 1990 it was a problem, with so much rebuilding going on that it had been rechristened *Barcelobra* – Barcelona building site. But the air of expectancy is contagious. I do not want to pretend that Barcelona is a perfect city. That is probably too much to ask of a city as it's too much to ask of a person. But when you live with a city over a period of years you become sensitive to how the thousands of tiny changes within a great city begin to coalesce into trends and movements. I have seen London become more divided, more uncared for, dirtier and more unhappy over twenty-five years. Over that same span I have seen Barcelona acquire a dynamic spirit which seems to me to set an agenda for the city of the year 2000.

The modern city is all about balance. People want to feel secure and safe in their own homes but they also want public spaces in which to mingle and feel involved with one another and with the great issues of our times. They want money in their pocket to spend as they will, but they also want good public services – buses and hospitals and schools. They want to feel part of the global village of telecommunications but they want to feel at home and comfortable in the intimate settings of family, street and neighbourhood. They want to experience themselves at the centre of the universe but also accept responsibility for their share in the earth's delicate ecology. Barcelona, I would suggest, is addressing these issues. London, I know, is not.

Chapter 9

The Language Question

In Wales and Scotland there are still numbers of people who speak the old Celtic languages of Welsh and Gaelic and for whom bilingualism is an everyday fact of life. Catalan nationalism is more clearly identified with a specific language and culture than is the case in either Wales or Scotland. Scottish Gaelic as an everyday language is confined to small areas of the northwest highlands and islands. The position of Welsh is much stronger, especially in the north and west, and there is substantial broadcasting in Welsh on both radio and television. Indeed, the closest we can come to understanding the problematic status of the Catalan language is in terms of those parts of North and West Wales, where the majority of the population are Welsh-speaking. Despite the lamentable lack of progress towards regional government, the Welsh language has had some success in challenging the dominant position of English in areas such as education and local government, and in the most visible area of road signs and other public notices. This progress has, in turn, been challenged from two directions. Firstly by immigrants from England, who see the Welsh language as archaic and of little value to them and their children. Secondly by militant separatists, who see the policy of bilingualism as implying the subordination of Welsh to English, and who link the language question to wider political issues related to their primary aim of political independence.

These same tendencies can be seen at work in Catalonia. But there is an initial complication which needs to be raised and it is the extent to which Catalan can be considered a totally separate language. When I went to live in Barcelona in 1968, there were considerable barriers to the use and development of Catalan. All public signs and documents, all education, all TV and radio, all the press and the vast majority of periodicals, and most publishing, were in Castilian Spanish. Yet most of my friends and most of the students I was teaching at the university spoke Catalan. I soon acquired sufficient facility to follow the main thread of an argument in Catalan and to use a few common expressions in the spoken language. I can now read almost as quickly in Catalan as in Castilian. Yet at no point can I say that I have learned to speak Catalan. And the reason is very clear. Given goodwill on both sides, Catalan and Castilian are mutually comprehensible. When I went out with large groups of people it was perfectly normal for the Catalans to speak Catalan and for those of us who did not speak it to join in the conversation in Castilian. This could not happen in either Wales or Scotland, because of the gulf between the English and the Celtic languages. By the same token, it is much easier for non-Catalan-speaking residents of Catalonia to acquire facility in the use of Catalan.

I am not arguing here that Catalan is a dialect. It is totally wrong to see the difference as merely the difference between English as spoken by a Glaswegian and a Londoner, or a white South African and a black West Indian. What I am saying about Catalan and Castilian is also true of Castilian and Portuguese or Italian, all of which derive from Latin. No-one challenges the right of these languages to be called languages, because of course we can identify Italy and Portugal as different nation states. Yet it is just an irony of history that Portugal, merged with the Spanish state from 1580 to 1640, was able to re-establish its national identity while the Catalans have spent most of that 350 years since 1640 under the thumb of Madrid. We confuse language group with nation state and one of the facts which has emerged from the tumultuous changes in Europe in very recent years is the extent to which language is not necessarily the arbiter of national identity. And while some multilingual states (Switzerland, Czechoslovakia) seem able to hang together relatively well, other such states (Belgium, Yugoslavia) do not. Clearly the reasons are political rather than linguistic.

While the Roman Empire still existed, the Latin language held together. Once the empire was out of the way, all that changed. In areas where the use of Latin had never had very deep roots (as in England) the language of the new settlers (Anglo-Saxon) took over. But in the areas that were later to become France, Spain, Italy and Romania, the local versions of 'vulgar' Latin (the Latin of the common people) began to diverge. Then, during the Middle Ages, as new states began to organise themselves, elements of standardisation began to reappear, especially as written forms of the new Romance languages emerged. There was also the tendency to use different languages for different purposes, a tradition which is still important when one considers how bilingual people behave on an hour-by-hour basis. So Catalan was both the spoken language of the people and the language of trade and commerce at the same time as Provençal was used for literature and Latin for the Church. It was not until the end of the medieval period that poets began to write in Catalan.

After the union of the crowns of Castile and Aragon, the use of Catalan for official and literary purposes went into decline. The appointment of non-Catalan bishops and clergy to Catalonia and the preaching of sermons in Castilian was one of the major grievances in the revolt of the Catalans in 1640 and the wars which ended in the Treaty of the Pyrenees (1659). Yet Catalan never disappeared as the spoken language of the people. Although Catalan institutions were abolished post–1714, and Catalan banned from official use, there was neither the systematic repression nor the massive emigration which put paid to the Gaelic language in Scotland. And as yet there was little immigration into Catalonia from other parts of Spain. So when the Romantic nationalists 'rediscovered' Catalan in the nineteenth century they had a very deep popular culture on which to draw for inspiration.

But until the middle of the nineteenth century, there is no doubt that Catalan was the 'low language' while Castilian was the language of both culture and power. An interesting reflection of this is the work of the Vilanova i La Geltrú poet Manuel de Cabanyes, who died in 1833. His work has been known in England for some time, with a book on his poetry published in Manchester by the well-known Hispanist and Ramon Llull scholar, E. Allison Peers, in 1923. Cabanyes came from the same kind of wealthy middle-class family as the *modernista* poet Joan Maragall (1860–1911), but whereas Maragall naturally wrote in Catalan, Cabanyes naturally wrote in Castilian. The key difference is the Industrial Revolution, which gave the Catalan middle class a distinct identity from that of the Castilian oligarchy who remained locked into a stagnant, almost feudal economy.

The *Renaixença* (Rebirth) lasted from 1833 to 1885, and built on the literary traditions of the Middle Ages, such as the *jocs florals* (floral games). The distant origins of the *jocs florals* are the Roman spring festivals which honoured the goddess Flora by garlanding her statues with flowers. Prizes were awarded to the poets who best honoured the arrival of spring. In the Middle Ages, the Provençal troubadours used the name *jocs florals* for their literary contests and in 1393 the first festival of this kind was held in Barcelona. Revived in 1859, these festivals became an integral part of the Catalan literary scene; the similarity of these Romantic nationalist events to the Eisteddfod movement in Wales is, I think, obvious. In the 1890s a similar format was adopted by the *festes modernistes*, held in Sitges under the direction of the author and painter Santiago Rusiñol.

Joan Maragall is the great poet of late nineteenth-century Catalonia, and of *Modernisme*. Verdaguer, the poet-priest of the *Renaixença*, had already established the notion of a poetry that went hand-in-hand with a spiritual exultation of the homeland of the Catalans in poems such as 'Canigó' and 'Montserrat'. Maragall wrote of the simple things of Catalonia, yet managed to charge them with a special significance, as in his poem 'L'Ametller' ('The almond-tree'):

> A mig aire de la serra
> Veig un ametller florit:
> Déu te guard, bandera blanca,
> Dies ha que t'he delit!
>
> Ets la pau que s'anuncia
> Entre el sol, núvols i vents . . .
> No ets encara el millor temps
> Pro en tens tota l'alegria.

(In the heart of the mountains / I can see an almond-tree in blossom: / Greetings, white flag, / I have missed you these last few days! / You have come to proclaim peace / between the sun, clouds and winds . . . / You are not yet the better weather / but you possess all its happiness.)

If in his poetry he aimed at spontaneity and sincerity, his substantial prose-work on social and political questions (much of it written in Castilian) was noticeable for preaching tolerance and understanding at a time of urban violence and periodic class warfare. This included the anarchist uprising of 1909 in Barcelona known as the Setmana Tràgica (Tragic Week). In his well-known poem to Barcelona, the 'Oda nova a Barcelona', he attempts to reconcile the conflicts of the city: 'Tal com ets, tal te vull, cuitat mala' (I want you just as you are, evil city.)

The nineteenth century established the Catalan language as an integral part of the claims of Catalan nationalism – national rights and national language hand-in-hand. The Mancomunitat (1916–24) reintroduced Catalan into local government and schools, and this process was intensified under the Generalitat from 1931. Under the leadership of the Mancomunitat, the spelling and grammar of Catalan were standardised and the freedom of expression enjoyed by a *modernista* poet such as Maragall replaced by the strict orthodoxy of the pipe-smoking poet, diplomat and translator, Josep Carner. Catalan had arrived as a language of power.

But it was the very success of the Catalan revival which made it certain that when Franco won the Civil War, radical steps would be taken to attack not only Catalan political rights but the language itself. Franquism made no distinction between the middle-class politicians of the Lliga and their socialist and communist counterparts. Carner as well as Casals tasted the bitter fruits of exile. For a short while after the war, it was an offence to speak Catalan in public places. There were signs in public phone boxes demanding that conversations took place in Castilian. For many years Catalan was banned from any kind of official use – in government offices, schools, universities, the media. And, of course, in the street where all road signs, advertising hoardings, shop signs, were in Castilian. Alistair Boyd writes that only twelve Catalan books were published in 1946, a figure that rose to 520 by 1968 and is now running at around 4,000 titles. In Vilanova, Xavier Garcia, who writes on local history, popular culture and the customs of the local fishermen, and always in Catalan, had to wait until the 1970s before any of his work was published. And this despite the fact that he had been writing regularly since 1940. He made his living by working in the offices of the Pirelli tyre factory and teaching Catalan as part of the firm's 'leisure-time' programme.

Although there has clearly been a revival in the use of Catalan since Franco's death in 1975, opinion remains divided about the actual state of health of Catalan. For one of the most significant linguistic events in Catalonia has been the arrival of large numbers of immigrants from other parts of Spain who speak Castilian as their only language. So there are whole districts in Barcelona and indeed in most industrial towns in Catalonia where it is a rarity to hear Catalan spoken. The fact is that all Catalans, except for some very small children, understand Castilian: the reverse is not the case. Thus there is a lot of social pressure on people to use Castilian. In a bar in Barcelona, the Catalan barman will address the customers in Castilian, unless he knows them personally. The same happens in shops and offices. This state of affairs, repeated throughout society, frequently leads to two Catalans using what is, for them, a foreign language for everyday purposes.

Joan Antoni Benach, who works for the Barcelona City Council as editor of their prestigious cultural magazine *Barcelona, Metròpolis Mediterrània*, was concerned about the general level of debate on the language question. In 1966 he had been one of the founders of the Grup Democràtic de Periodistes (Democratic Journalists Group), which had as one of its chief objectives the increased use of Catalan in the mass media. Benach felt that there was a risk of self-satisfaction on the part of politicians about the progress that has been achieved in recent years. He cited the question of television. Yes, there is Catalan television, but the audience has in fact gone down, and the actual proportion of television in Catalan diminished since the recent opening of two new independent commercial stations. At the same time he also insisted that offering programmes such as 'Dallas' and 'Eastenders' in Catalan had 'broken down psychological barriers' and taken away the idea of Catalan as merely a linguistic oddity.

The policy of the Generalitat that receives most general support from Catalan politicians of all parties is the policy of 'linguistic normalisation'. As I noted during my brief excursion into France, the first thing you notice is that all public signs tend to be in French. In Catalonia it is now rare to see a road sign in Castilian. Alistair Boyd, in the mid-1980s, found Lleida's street names half in Castilian, half in Catalan. Now they are all in Catalan. Only in Girona was there any evidence of opposition, with graffitti which asked for 'Spanish please', copying the familiar 'In Catalan please' slogan of the linguistic nationalists. More controversial is the general use of Catalan in public notices, such as warnings about the dangers of forest fires. But it is at this point that the closeness of Catalan to Castilian comes in. It does not actually take much of a leap of the imagination to recognise repeated signs in Catalan, even if it isn't the language you speak at home. Even where the word is quite different the context usually makes the meaning clear. Barcelona is a city of slogans. 'Barcelona som tots' (Barcelona is all of us) is close enough to the Castilian 'Barcelona somos todos' to be immediately recognised, and also to promote the language as a factor of integration rather than separation. Similarly, a closed shop is closed whether the sign says 'tancat' or 'cerrado'! And since both Catalan and Castilian are recognised as official languages, all government offices dealing with the public will use the language which comes most naturally to the client.

But for some of the most enthusiastic nationalists I know, the language can still be a problem, especially the written language. People who went to school between about 1940 and 1980 can only read and write Catalan if they made a special effort to learn it outside school. Thus the statistics about the use of Catalan differ according to whether you are asking how many people understand, speak, read, or write it, the figures declining in that order. While most people understand Catalan (including those not born in Catalonia or born into Castilian-speaking families), only a minority of Catalans can write their own language with any fluency. However, one of the ironies of the present position is that all these figures are higher than in the Basque country, yet Basque separatism has for twenty years been a cause of political extremism and violence while Catalan nationalism has tended to be relatively peaceful. The apparently contradictory explanations are, on the one hand, the very repressed state of the Basque culture and language and, on the other hand, that immigrants to the Basque country have found assimilation much easier because the language is much less used. There is more intermarriage, for example. Another factor is, of course, that Catalan nationalism, with its strong emphasis on the language and culture, is a matter of some indifference to the non-Catalan working class. This helps to explain the stranglehold that the conservative nationalists of CiU maintain on the Generalitat in a country with a long tradition of working-class militancy.

There is no doubt that education is a crucial issue. And it is here that what politicians desire and what is feasible in practice can come into sharp conflict. In the Franco years, the imposition of Castilian as the universal medium of instruction was imposed with the full support of the press, radio and later television in Castilian, plus the existence within Catalonia of several million people for whom Castilian was the first or only language. During the debate on the 1970 Education Law, the official view was put that, 'Language is not just the vehicle by which people communicate, because through it is filtered the soul, and, sometimes, the viruses of the soul.' The suggestion was, of course, that Catalan nationalism was one such 'virus of the soul'. The pre-democratic town halls of both Girona and Barcelona voted in 1975 against allocating funds for the teaching of Catalan in local schools.

Yet, despite the legacy of the dictatorship, the use of Catalan at school, a major political demand in the years of transition, has become a central plank of linguistic normalisation. This is now beginning to work through the school system. Thus we can say with some confidence that a primary school will be Catalan-speaking, while in a secondary school it varies from school to school and even from subject to subject. At university level, the balance again varies from one department to another.

One major problem has had to be faced. Children are expected to use Catalan at school from the start, though for some of them brought up in predominantly immigrant communities, this may be their first real contact with the language. They learn to read and write in Catalan, and only later is Castilian introduced. The aim is for each child to become fluent in both languages. The risk, of course, is that they may become fluent in neither. An old friend of mine in Barcelona asked me how I would feel if my children were starting school in a language that was not my own. She describes herself as a 'Castilian-speaking Catalan'. When I recounted this to other friends, their retort was, well how did she think they had felt during all those years when Catalan-speaking children had been taught at school in a foreign language?

By and large, there is multiparty support for the linguistic policy, both in general terms and as applied to education. But there is great scope for political backbiting and point-scoring. Thus the socialists deride the chauvinism of the nationalists and the nationalists accuse the socialists of not being really committed to the Catalan cause. Part of the problem would seem to be the confusion between political nationalism and the linguistic revival. Shorn of the nationalist rhetoric, the linguistic normalisation policy seems an eminently sensible plan to restore the cultural identity of Catalonia. But the nationalist rhetoric can encourage at home a narrow view of nation that does not take account of non-Catalan speakers, and in the rest of Spain and abroad a hostility to what can often appear like narrow chauvinism.

One particularly interesting part of the language question is the field of Catalan publishing and literature. Out of a total of up to 4,000 titles now appearing annually in Catalan, a sizable minority have been published by the Generalitat, about a thousand in its first decade 1980–90. Josep-Maria Puigjaner, who is in charge of the Generalitat's publishing department, explained to me that the aim was to fill a hole in what was available commercially. There are a few popular successes, tourist books which also appear in Castilian and other common European languages, but many of the books are specialist texts in Catalan in subjects such as history and culture, science and technology. This form of state enterprise allows print runs of 1,500–3,000, with each department contributing to the list in areas of public life it is responsible for. This means that titles such as *Tobacco Abuse in Catalonia*, *Catalonia in the World Transport Context* and *Energy Saving in Building Design* all appear under the Generalitat imprint, as well as a light-hearted picture dictionary called *Holidays in Catalonia*, which I found extremely useful in improving my own knowledge of day-to-day Catalan.

The Spanish monarchy, at least in the person of the heir to the Spanish throne, Prince Philip, is very supportive of the Catalan language. Indeed, during his 1990 trip to Catalonia, the Prince repeatedly used the vocabulary of federalism to describe the reality of Spain as the sum total of its parts. He urged the Catalan nation to retain its own special identity of which the language was an important part. As Joan Barril, a columnist on *El País*, commented on St George's Day, the words 'Catalan nationality' come much more readily to the lips of the Prince than to the lips of Prime Minister Felipe González. In addressing the Catalan parliament the Prince used both Castilian and Catalan. He referred to the 'Spain of the nationalities and of their cultures in their variety and unity'. But there are subtleties here which can escape the notice of the innocent traveller. 'Nationality' means national identity rather than a political unit. Pierre Vilar, a French historian of Catalonia, has written of 'the historical dialectic between *nationality*, a long-term fact, *nationalism*, a restless aware-

117

ness, and *nation*, a politically organised group'. Part of the 'long-term fact' of Catalonia is now precisely its linguistic and cultural complexity.

In April 1990, I saw in a shop-window in Barcelona a few pages of an ephemeral Catalan magazine published in New York in 1874. There was a cartoon strip story of a meeting between a Catalan peasant and Uncle Sam. It went like this:

Uncle Sam: What the hell language is that?
Mr Ambrós: Catalan, mate, don't you recognise it?
Uncle Sam: Catalan! What's that?
Mr Ambrós: What do you mean, 'that'! Show more respect, it's the universal language.

Uncle Sam then explains that the universal language is English, to which Mr Ambrós replies by asking whether any English language magazines are published in Spain:

Uncle Sam: No.
Mr Ambrós: Well, here's one in Catalan published in New York.

It is difficult to know exactly how many people speak Catalan. Of the six million inhabitants of Catalonia, probably two-thirds speak the language, with a lower figure of those who can read it as well. Even adding in the Catalan speakers of France, Valencia and the Balearic Islands, the figure of ten million given by Alistair Boyd seems optimistic, while the twenty million of the Generalitat's *This is Catalonia* is clearly wrong.

Bilingualism is an everyday fact of life in Catalonia. Catalan is important because it is the language which affirms national identity and culture. Castilian is important because it is one of the great international languages, the second language of the USA and the main language (with the exception of Portuguese in Brazil) of the whole of Latin America. Yet it is not acceptable to see Catalan as the domestic language for local purposes and Castilian as the public language of international communication, because it implies a subordination of Catalan to its larger neighbour. Languages are about power as well as about culture. So far, the case for Catalan as a language of the European Community has met with little success. This is not surprising as the linguistic complexities of the EC are already very great and likely to become greater as new countries join. Just as there is a logic about German economic influence in the EC, so there is a logic about the use of English as the European language. As long as Spain exists, Castilian will be an important means of communication in Catalonia. But if only Europe existed, then Catalans and Castilians might well one day find themselves talking to one another in English.

Within Catalonia itself the argument for bilingualism rests not so much on the question of communication with the rest of Spain or even Latin America, but on the rights of the large minority for whom Castilian is a first language. Their rights and their culture will only be defended in the medium term by an active policy of bilingualism at all levels of society. In the longer term some form of assimilation would appear to be inevitable. But this will only have a divisive political edge if the Catalan government continues to tolerate, if not actively to support, the more extreme claims of 'linguistic nationalism'.

Chapter 10

Popular Culture

The Catalan notion of popular culture has some affinities with
the English notion of folklore. Except that English folklore is
almost entirely something artificial, preserved by special groups,
and having strong antiquarian and rather quirky overtones. Apart
from a few survivals such as well-dressing in Derbyshire, there is
little sense of continuity with the pre-industrial past. That is not
the case in Catalonia. Industrialisation came later and left large
areas of the country untouched until very recent years. People
who emigrated to the big cities were far more likely to retain links
with their native village and go back home for local holidays and
celebrations. In Vilanova i La Geltrú, on the Catalan coast
between Barcelona and Tarragona, there is a continuing tradition
of popular celebrations which are public rather than private in
character and usually take place in the open air. In addition there
is an annual international festival of folk music, a lot of which is
folklore in the English sense of the word. A number of local
experts have written extensively on the history of traditional
festivities and in most cases these researches have fed back into
the way these festivities are celebrated in the present.

Popular culture does not exclude involvement in other kinds of
culture. The same young people who take part in Carnaval
processions and dances also enjoy international pop music. Many
of them are also fanatical followers of Barcelona Football Club. In
the 1970s the success of FC Barcelona became a matter of as much
public concern as the Catalan statute of autonomy. Vilanova, like
most towns in Catalonia, has its Barcelona Supporters' Club,
decked out in the blue and red colours synonymous with the
team. As Terry Venables found during his years at the Nou
Camp, it is a national symbol as well as a great football club.
Anything less than total success, as Venables found, is not
tolerated. A group of *castellers* (human castle-builders) meeting

on a Friday evening had to change the time of their meeting to fit in with an especially popular TV quiz show that none of the members wanted to miss. Their involvement in the popular culture has to be understood as representing a particular part of their lives, namely their desire to be actively involved in the cause of national identity. I talked about this to the grandly titled Cultural Councillor of Vilanova, socialist politician, Sixte Moral. A handsome man in an open-neck shirt, his dark hair tied back in a neat knot, he is the charismatic focus of popular cultural activity in the town. 'Our intention,' he said, 'is to break with the idea of the individual consumer of culture sitting in front of a television set. What we are trying to do, on the contrary, is to encourage people to relate together in public spaces as one part of living together and participation.'

The cause of popular culture over the past fifty years has followed a parallel course to that of the language. That is to say that an initial attempt to clamp down on popular festivities was gradually replaced by what can best be described as repressive tolerance. Some concessions were made, but the policy was still firmly to keep the lid on cultural nationalism as much as on political nationalism. The main beneficiary of this was the *sardana*. In retrospect, my life in Barcelona was full of *sardanas*. Sunday evening in the Plaça Sant Jaume was always one of my favourite haunts, especially during my first year there. Later I remember waking in my room above a bakery in the old town to the strains of the *cobla* band from the square in front of the cathedral where *sardanas* are danced at midday on Sunday. Or, if I had got up to go to a concert at the Palau, wandering past and stopping for a few minutes en route for the bars and restaurants down towards the port. Even during the state of emergency in the winter of 1968/9, when any meeting of more than three or four people was potentially an illegal act, *sardana* dancing went on. There is something strong and powerful about it: the linked hands always in a circle, the symbolic protest of a repressed people.

Religious festivals continued, too, but with a strong emphasis on their religious as opposed to their civil elements, since many of these religious festivals overlayed earlier pagan celebrations. But the Franco regime, depending heavily as it did on traditional Catholicism for its shoestring legitimacy, was always out to humour the Church. What was omitted was the ludic (playful) aspect of the Catalan *festa*. Carnaval, with its connotations of

121

sexual intrigue as well as over-indulgence in food and drink, suffered particularly badly. Its survival in places like Vilanova owes as much to business as to folklore. The same applies to traditional markets such as the Christmas market in front of the cathedral in Barcelona, which sells Christmas trees, decorations, candles, and especially the carved wooden figures for the crib which most Catalan families have in their homes at Christmas, or the market of Sant Ponç in Barcelona, when herbs, honey and fruit preserves are sold at stalls in the Hospital Street in the old town. Moral reckons that at Carnaval in Vilanova 5–6,000 people are spending up to 60,000 pesetas (£350) each on clothes, partying and so on.

The government attempted to trivialise and sentimentalise popular culture by turning it into a tourist attraction in which a few local people would perform for the benefit of an audience consisting largely of outsiders. Yet the reality was a popular culture that continued to express political protest. This can clearly be seen in the Barcelona celebrations of Sant Jordi. The linking of Saint George and the red rose tradition with national book day allowed an official view to develop which was more like St Valentine's Day: the man gives his beloved a rose, and the woman gives the man a book. The link is not entirely contrived. The Roman Floral Games, revived by the medieval troubadours and the nineteenth-century cultural nationalists, linked flowers to poetry through the prizes awarded for the best verses of welcome for spring. But as with the *sardana*, the actual way in which people understood their participation in these rituals was very different.

In a lengthy interview I conducted with Josep Maria Ainaud de Lasarte, a senior CiU (conservative nationalist) councillor in Barcelona, he proudly claimed to have been the first to hang a Catalan flag in the Generalitat Palace during an April 23rd celebration, when the whole palace is traditionally decorated with red roses. His view of Sant Jordi as the protector of the weak against the strong has a clear local political resonance. But this political aspect has been rapidly lost in the transition to democracy. Sixte Moral claimed that, 'A display of *castellers* or *sardanas* or a *festa major* no longer embodies a spirit of protest, it's simply a ludic, participatory, festive spectacle.' Nevertheless, 23 April is still a wonderful day to be in Catalonia. The streets are lined with stalls selling books and roses, and there is a special

122

sense of excitement in the air. In Barcelona's *rambla*, books and roses now have to compete with a variety of other interest groups who take advantage of Sant Jordi to set up stalls: gays, greens, assorted groups of nationalists and the usual array of left-wing fringe groups. Later on in the evening there are some ritualistic disturbances and window-smashing to show that the spirit of protest is still alive in Barcelona.

Popular culture related first of all to rural life and the importance of the seasons in agriculture. So each season had its festival. Christmas and the midwinter celebrations are more familiar to us in Northern Europe, but in Catalonia the tradition is that the Three Kings bring children presents on 6 January (Epiphany). This is complemented in rural areas by other traditions that give priority to Christmas Day, or the days of Saint Nicholas, Saint Catherine or Santa Llúcia, whose *festa* is celebrated by the Barcelona Christmas market. Christmas in Catalonia is in a state of flux. At the Santa Llúcia market traditional wooden figures for the family crib are sold alongside cheap plastic ones and gaudy Christmas decorations. Christmas cards have made an appearance in the last twenty-five years, but it is not considered necessary to send cards to people you never see or to offer gifts to distant relations you neither see nor even like. The greatest effort, as with all Catalan celebrations, goes into the family meal, usually shared by different generations and branches of the family according to the limits of the dining-room table. Traditional Catalan cooking concentrates heavily on meat, fish, poultry, game and fresh vegetables, and the complicated sauces that distinguish French cooking are not greatly favoured. Sparkling wine from the Penedès (*cava*) is the most popular drink, though in recent years improved wine-making methods have begun to show results in dry whites and full-bodied reds that can compete with the best in Europe.

The Lent cycle of festivals includes Els Tres Tombs, when animals are brought to church for blessing, and the controversial Carnaval, which has always been a source of dispute between Church and civil society. It includes, for example, the character of the King of Fools, who preaches a 'sermon' to the people which is usually a satire on the local authorities. There are also dancing, feasting and processions. Carnaval in Vilanova involves a full week of celebrations from the last Thursday in Lent until Ash Wednesday. The King of Fools arrives on the Friday to read his sermon, and on Ash Wednesday he is 'buried'. His 'will' is then read, usually continuing the satirical vein of the sermon. There are four days of masked dances and street processions that feature battles between groups armed with sweets. The sweets do less damage than the chunks of plaster used in the eighteenth century, which were eventually banned by the town council because of the number of injuries.

Easter is the time of rebirth and growth, and the story of Christ rising from the dead is complemented by the greenery that accompanies the Palm Sunday processions. This has very ancient roots. In Greece and Rome there was a festival at about this time, dedicated to the laurel and the olive. The olive and its oil was basic to the economy of the ancient world, and the tree lived to an incredible age, while the laurel was much used in cooking and reputed to have special properties such as warding off lightning. The crown of laurels was the classical symbol of victory. The rich food which marked the ending of Lent is reflected in the Easter Egg, whose modern chocolate form is traditionally given to children by their godparents, a tradition that survives even in non-religious families.

After Easter comes the cycle of the tree and the rose, the ancient Roman Floral Games. This is reflected in the rose of Sant Jordi, maypoles, which are still relatively common in Catalonia, floral carpets in Sitges and the Corpus celebrations. Corpus was an explicit attempt in medieval Europe to provide a Christian alternative to the pagan celebrations associated with spring and their *geni*. Corpus in Barcelona was a big civic event which shared many of the characters more familiar to visitors to Catalonia from the summer *festa major* – the giants, the animals (mules, dragons, etc.) and the stick dances very close to our own Morris Dance. Something of the rich diversity of Corpus in fifteenth-century Barcelona can be gleaned from listing just some of the parts of the procession passing down Montcada Street: trumpeters, flags, candlesticks, craft guilds, crosses, clergy, religious orders, tableaux of the Creation and Hell, devils, angels, figures dressed up as David and Goliath, Cain and Abel, the Three Wise Men, saints and martyrs, a dragon and an eagle.

Most seaports in Catalonia have their own distinctive festivities. Vilanova celebrates St Peter, the patron saint of fishermen, on 29 June. The highlight is a procession of 40–50 boats decorated with flags around the harbour, carrying an image of the saint.

124

The night before there is a party on the beach, with *coca*, sweet wine and dancing. Local historian Xavier Garcia told me that this tradition is over one hundred years old, but that in recent years it has become part of a 'Sea Week', with talks, music, dancing, swimming races and exhibitions about maritime customs. He also explained to me how much of the folklore of the sea has become part of the vivid imagery of the language. So 'aferrar-se com un pop' (to cling on like an octopus) comes to mean taking up a strong doctrinal or political position.

The *festa major* of August or September had its origins in the harvest festivals. Indeed, some inland villages where olives are the main traditional crop have their *festa major* in winter. This is reflected in two particular ways, both of which stress collective endeavour, which was essential to the successful harvest. These are the *sardana*, with its origins lost in the circle dances common in the ancient world, and the castle-building. The *castellers* had their high point in the late nineteenth century in the coastal districts of New Catalonia, but the vigorous modern revival shows signs of spreading more widely. It involves people of different ages, including the young children who clamber up on top, men and, in the modern period increasingly, women. The base of the castle is where the members of the group mingle and lend their individual strength to the common endeavour. The *castellers* have been particularly successful in attracting the 'new' Catalans, immigrants and the children of immigrants, into their ranks. Moral saw this integrative aspect of popular culture as very important in building the new Catalonia. He pointed to the irony that very few of the children who perform the frightening task of being the summit of the castle are actually from Catalan-speaking families!

Much of the information in the past couple of pages is from a book published in 1980 by Benve Moya, the director of the Teatre Principal in Vilanova, a slight, balding figure with a humorous moustache and twinkling eyes. He has spent a lifetime in the theatre, and chooses to work in a small town like Vilanova because he likes the small scale of it. But he commented to me in his snug little office by the stage door that it is not 'provincial' in the derogatory sense of the word. He keeps in touch with the Barcelona cultural scene through journalism, reading and going to the theatre (Barcelona is only about forty-five minutes away by train). His own reputation was substantially formed as a member

125

of the famous mime group Els Joglars, who were never Barcelona-based, working around the provinces from one small town to another. In Vilanova he has found other people interested in what I would describe as 'active' research on popular culture, aimed not at an academic audience but at increasing the authenticity and the popular appeal of popular culture. It was noticeable how this group, unprompted by me, often came out with very similar formulations about the importance of popular culture as a social and political statement in the Franquist period, the importance of public, participatory art, the human scale of street festivals. Moya's point about the unprovincial nature of Vilanova is reinforced by the annual international folk music festival, which attracts 7–8,000 people for events which would simply not find an audience in Barcelona.

Popular culture in a town like Vilanova is very different from the 'official' version put out by the Generalitat, because the Generalitat stresses the exceptional or out-of-the-ordinary, but fails to stress the importance of taking over public spaces for these activities, a point all my Vilanova contacts were at pains to emphasise, and fails to address the interests and involvement of the 'new' Catalans. It also takes an excessive interest in the *sardana*. The main complaint I heard in Vilanova against the *sardana* was from Xavier Orriols, a musicologist who is actively involved in the popular culture movement. He felt, for example, that the strict nature of the dance limited the potential of the band, the *cobla*. It does seem curious that these bands play no other music at all. Orriols thought that musically it had stagnated. Anthony Baines, an English writer on folk music, claimed in a scholarly article in 1953 that, 'A European town in the sixteenth century must have sounded like present-day Barcelona or Girona on a Sunday morning.' Yet Orriols demonstrated to me that only the smallest pipe, the *flabiol*, has retained its original form, with the tenor with its mechanical keys taking over as 'king of the *cobla*'. Indeed the use of wind instruments themselves was a sixteenth-century innovation, replacing the bagpipes which are still found in their primitive form in Mallorca. The music of New Catalonia was dominated not by the *sardana cobla* but by the *gralla*, another type of simple pipe instrument. It is this instrument which now dominates popular festivals in Vilanova, played to accompany the *castellers*, or in public processions.

It was the thin clear notes of the *gralla* that went on echoing through my head long after the smoke and noise and confusion of the *festa major* procession in Vilanova had passed in August 1990. It was a grey leaden afternoon of intense heat which never quite concentrated itself enough to produce the expected thunderstorm. We were invited to join the local dignitaries on the balcony of the town hall, where the processions end, but we preferred to stay in the *rambla*. Proceedings began calmly enough with a brass band concert which entertained us as we sat sipping iced coffee and lemon juice and *horchata*, an odd but extremely thirst-quenching milky drink produced from the roots of plants which is common all over Spain in summer. By six p.m. the chairs had all been cleared away and groups of dancers were gathering, each in the distinctive costume of their particular club. Each cultural group (*castellers*, stick-dance, dragon, etc.) is run independently and often these clubs have a meeting place to practise which also serves as a social centre. The heat hangs like an enormous awning over the town. By seven p.m. the crowd of strollers had thickened to a stream, affluent-looking people in their Sunday best with carefully groomed children anxious for ice creams and balloons and excitement.

Conversation reaches a crescendo of excitement as drum rolls and fire crackers announce the arrival of the procession at the head of the *rambla*.

'They're coming, they're coming.'

'The dragon's on its way!'

'Watch out for the little devils.'

'That poor dog's terrified.'

'Move over a bit, I can't see.'

For the next hour this immense tableau unfurls itself past us. We are soon forced to retreat from our vantage point at a pavement café by the little devils with their whirling sticks of fire, their faces painted black, and their multicoloured costumes with red tails and horns. A black spaniel flees in terror and a few small children dissolve into tears. Already blue-grey smoke is drifting down the *rambla* in advance of the fire-spouting dragons, with their supporting casts of musicians, wearing the traditional white trousers and shirts with black sashes.

These representations of semimythical beasts, already part of the medieval Corpus processions, carried by one or more people, are both very ancient in form and very modern in content. The most typical beast of Vilanova is the mule (*la mulassa*) which

127

comes later in the procession. Where dragons, the commonest beasts in this part of Catalonia, represent the dark side of nature, the mule is nature tamed, domestic but high-spirited with a keen sense of comedy. It prances to and fro across the *rambla*, charging the crowds, nosing into women's handbags and taking the occasional crafty nip at the person leading it. It dances to the traditional tunes of the bull-fighting festivals in Pamplona in distant Navarre, and has the largest *gralla* and drum band and the most fervent support from the home crowd. Vilanova certainly had a mule as early as 1629, which behaved more like a dragon until, in 1779, it was banned from breathing fire and fire crackers following a similar ban in Barcelona in 1771. Unfortunately, together with the giants and dragon of Vilanova, it found itself stranded in Barcelona in July 1936 at a Pueblo Español (Spanish Village) festival and these popular figures became some of the more bizarre victims of the Civil War.

Some of the noisiest figures of the procession, dressed in knee britches, waistcoats and red floppy Catalan berets which always remind me of Father Christmas costumes, are the musketeers of the Ball d'en Serrallonga (Serrallonga dance). This is a most curious historical relic which began as a play and has ended up as a dance. It purports to tell the story of a group of Catalan bandits, led by Joan de Serrallonga, who roamed the hills of Catalonia, more admired for their daring, chivalry and courage than condemned for their lawless existence. The dancers alternate between ear-splitting volleys from their antique muskets and a dance of extreme intricacy, pausing to recite some of the rhetorical verses of the original drama. As their tale of blood and thunder fades down towards the sea in a haze of fire and smoke, the local giants have formed up opposite one another at the top of the *rambla*. These enormous figures perform a stately and very formal dance which gradually moves down the *rambla*. They represent two couples, one aristocratic, the other peasant, and a further regal couple wearing Moorish turbans. The district of La Geltrú, one half of this twin town, celebrates a separate *festa major* but its giants also take part in the Vilanova processions. The giants represent formality and gentility after the excesses of dragons and mules. The Vilanova ones are fortunate in being able to make dignified entrances into the town hall, which has an extremely high grand entrance. At Mataró, at the end of each *festa major*, there has developed an intricate ceremony called putting the giants to bed, since they can only be got in and out of the town hall lying on their backs.

Musically, the procession is extremely varied. The traditional dances and figures are accompanied by the *gralla* and drum, but there is also the town band and a children's band, plus the band from Vilarreal, Vilanova's 'twin town' in Valencia, which had given the sedate teatime concert. Other musicians take the opportunity to show off traditional instruments. I see Xavier Orriols going past with his bagpipes, and another unlikely ensemble consisting of trumpet, drum, bagpipe and *gralla*. There are numerous groups of children dancing with hoops and sticks, and the crowd at times breaks ranks to form up around a particular group, parting again to allow them to pass on down the *rambla*. The gipsy dancers I had watched meeting two hours earlier turn up as maypole dancers with a castanet accompaniment.

By now the heat is beginning to take its toll, and some of the dancers, the children especially, are looking quite exhausted. But of course the *festa major* lasts for several days, and all of these groups will be out again in the morning for a further procession round the town. In addition, the small pipe and drum groups will be going round the town at eight o'clock the following morning to remind people that the *festa major* is on – a fact hard to miss. In Mataró this reminder begins at dawn and is accompanied by the setting off of fireworks in the streets. It is the only time in my life I have woken up certain that World War III had started. At sunset the *castellers* perform in the Plaça de la Vila and conditions are perfect for the night-time firework display which attracts enormous crowds to the harbour at eleven o'clock. And still the party goes on. There is an all-night dance in the park by the beach. By one o'clock the temperature has dropped to just 30°C. The red moon sinks into the sea and the red sun rises out of it, with the fish eagerly gobbling flies on the limp flat surface of the water.

Summer is festival time in Catalonia, though not all festivals have the authentic feel of Vilanova. In the larger towns, Girona and Barcelona, summer activities are more cosmopolitan and varied, appealing both to traditional popular culture, but also to the international cultures of classical and popular entertainment. The Barcelona summer festival, the Grec, lasts from late June until August. It features theatre and dance at the open-air 'Greek' theatre on Montjuïc, which gives the festival its name, and at the Mercat de Flors (the old flower market turned cultural centre), concerts in the Plaça del Rei in the Old Town of classical, folk and rock music, and large-scale pop concerts at the Velodrome in Horta. On a more local scale, districts such as Nou Barris hold dances, concerts, films, sporting events, fireworks and a whole series of out-of-school events and outings for children. Here commercial sponsorship and public service go hand-in-hand.

One of the more interesting events in the summer of 1990 in Barcelona was the *festa major* of the Raval, the area between the *rambla* and Montjuïc which includes the traditional red-light district of the Chinese Quarter. Here the encouragement of popular events is linked to the planning policy of reviving this old district by thinning out the densities, creating new open spaces and generally renovating the urban structure – housing, car parking, pavements and so on. Not to mention increased police activity to try to eradicate the drugs problem which is endemic here. This has the wholehearted support of the neighbourhood association but it is an uphill struggle. Barcelona has long been a major entry point into Europe of the drug trade, especially hashish from North Africa. I was warned not to venture into the Raval alone at night, but I have to say that I feel safe in Barcelona in a way that I don't always in London. There are always so many people on the street, and a sense of safety in numbers without which many of the open-air events would be impossible.

The *festa major* coincided with the inauguration of the brand new Plaça de les Caramelles. Activities included dances, theatre, cabaret, fireworks and a performance of *habaneres*, music named after La Havana in Cuba that reflects the long association between Catalonia and the old Spanish colonies. Many of the coastal towns, especially of the Maresme, the coast between Barcelona and the Costa Brava, have these groups, playing a form of Latin American music which has become an integral part of Catalan popular culture.

In Girona, I was fortunate that my arrival from France in July coincided with one of a series of open-air concerts held on the steps of the cathedral. Or rather the performers occupy the *plaça* at the foot of the steps with the audience assembled up the great staircase that leads to the façade of the cathedral. Surprisingly for Girona in July, it was a cloudy evening, with the rain just holding off for the duration of the concert, and a mischievous wind making off with sheet music and music stands. On each quarter the cathedral bells join in with the music. The performer was Ovidi Montllor, whose music was already popular among university students in the late 1960s. Some of the audience were people of that generation, but many were much younger, for he has managed both musically and culturally to stay in the mainstream of Catalan music, as well as developing a career as a stage and film actor. Some of the texts were poetry rather than song, and he has made a speciality of musical adaptations of the remarkable 'anarchist' poet Joan Salvat-Papasseit, whose early death from the classic poets' disease of consumption in 1924 robbed the Catalan avant-garde of a voice which might have matched the paintings of Picasso, Dalí and Miró. Papasseit came from the working class and his writings include pamphlets and manifestos in which the idea of rebellion is exalted as what Alan Yates, the best-known Catalan scholar in the UK, calls 'a creative and spiritual adventure'. His books of poetry include *Poemes en ondes hertzianes* (*Radio wave poems*) of 1919, with a cover by Torres García which depicts a radio mast high above a city of factories, trains and trams. The influence of Italian Futurism is patent.

Back in Barcelona, it is Gràcia that offers the most lively and the most traditional *festa major*. A lot of this takes place in and around the Plaça Sol, a popular meeting place for artists and intellectuals but also a haven in a bustling, turbulent city on any day in the year. Barcelona has always been a city of banners and slogans, even in Franco's days, and the current one on a sultry Sunday afternoon in July was 'Mans unides: campanya contra la fam' (Join hands against world hunger). There are roller skaters and skate-boarders, children and parents, groups of young men and women, and a lot of Sunday papers in evidence. This very English tradition seems to be catching hold even in a country where the press has never had the prestige and importance, not to mention the jingoistic vulgarity, of its English counterpart. Beneath the plane trees and the palms, people come and go. A deeply sunburnt girl in a flouncy black Andalusian dress, earrings and a turquoise silk scarf round her bare shoulders arrives and as quickly departs the Café del Sol. The waiter, his dark hair tied back in a tidy knot, assumes the same leisurely pace as most of his customers. At the prices the café charges no-one is in a hurry to down their drinks, jump up and leave.

131

It is this acceptance of life in the open air in all its complexity, its conflicts and its many pleasures, this sense of public spaces as a natural extension of home and theatre and committee room, which provides the natural context for the flowering of popular culture.

Chapter 11

Mass Tourism (Sea, Sun and Sex)

The impulse that has led millions of Britons to Catalonia in recent years is easy enough to understand. Unfortunately, it has little to do with Catalonia and everything to do with the rigours of the British climate. Writing these lines on a damp, cold, cheerless New Year's Eve in London, and revising them in the middle of London's heaviest snowstorm for years, the urge to escape is overwhelming. The papers, the television advertisements, are full of exciting suggestions, most of which seem to boil down to three things – sea, sun and sex – with a supply of cheap booze thrown in for good measure. All of these the Spanish costas provided, except perhaps the sex, but that is an easily exportable commodity.

The times they are changing, though. There is uncertainty in the package holiday business. There is an overall reduction in volume of holidays sold in Britain, from over twelve million in 1988 to a little over nine million in 1990. In only one year, 1989–90, the proportion of those holidays taken at Spanish resorts (mainland, Balearics, Canaries and Catalonia) has declined from forty-five to thirty-four per cent. In the summer of 1990, the weather was considerably more reliable in England than in Catalonia – witness the frequent references in this book to thunderstorms – but that cannot explain such a major shift in people's habits. And while the future of package tour operators in the UK is a rather minor aspect of the recession, what happens to tourism in Catalonia is of paramount importance to the Catalans.

It is the coast and not the interior regions which has both enjoyed and suffered the impact of the migratory hordes. At Easter 1969, as I mentioned in the preface, I walked the northern part of the Costa Brava, from L'Escala to Port de la Selva. I noted even at Easter, 'the Germans, the French and the Belgians thundering to and fro in search of pleasure'. I noted the new development of Empúriabrava, a kind of Venice laid out on the drained and canalised marshes south of Roses, which contrasted favourably with the 'ugly square blocks giving on to dirty sand'. I visited the beach at Canyelles Petites on the other side of Roses, picking my way first through the maquis scrub and then through the new villas of the most recent urbanisation. Josep Pla, whose guide to the Costa Brava I was carrying in my rucksack, wrote that there was a fishing hut there. The kindly owner of the bar-restaurant, one of the first houses to be built at Canyelles, showed me a picture postcard of eight years previously with only three or four houses. But within a few minutes I was wandering the wild, flowery cliffs towards Punta Falconera and Cap de Norfeu, with a smooth turquoise sea (the only such sea I saw on that particular trip) far beneath me. The main obstruction on that walk was not tourist installations but a military zone, which forced me to retreat from the coast to the official 'picturesque' path inland.

Pla and Macaulay both write of a coast which was unspoilt but in many ways backward, a coastline which had not shared in the prosperity of Catalan trade and industry but which was sharing fully the trials and tribulations of Franquist Spain, cut off from the rest of Europe, denied American aid, and denied any sense of its national cultural identity by a centralist and authoritarian regime. In Cadaqués, Macaulay met a waiter who had worked for ten years in New York and remembered reading that many Cadaqués men emigrate to America, 'because life in Cadaqués is hard'. As if the life of fishing people had ever been anything else! Potentially, then, tourism brought a welcome diversification of economic activity, but already in 1969 it was obvious that its blessings were mixed. Alongside the urbanisations and the villas were springing up the first of the tower block hotels. By 1969 the Franco government had been captured by very different interests, eager to promote economic development and disdainful of any kind of controls. In particular, they rejected planning, the only hope for an orderly development of the Catalan coast.

How bad the results are is a subjective question. Take Tossa, for example, which Macaulay described as 'the most interesting and beautiful of the Costa Brava towns'. She admitted that it had been a 'picturesque resort of English writers and artists' before the Civil War, but declared herself satisfied with a town that 'has everything' – adding (in parenthesis) 'except those smart amenities believed to attract tourists'. Tossa today is full of amenities. Arriving by car on an August morning, I was immediately aware of what a well-ordered resort it was. Cars are carefully funnelled into one of a number of municipal car parks on or near the seafront but well screened from it:

'I'm sorry, senyor, you can't park here.'

'Why not? It's a car park, isn't it?'

'But you are not a car. You are a van. I am sorry, you must find another place.'

My campervan was politely rejected, presumably on the basis that I might decide to try to camp there, and I had to find a parking spot away from the sea, thus 'saving' myself 650 pesetas.

It would be hard to find fault with modern Tossa, unless you were looking for solitude. The beach, which is one of a number on this coast boasting European blue flag status, is busy but not uncomfortably crowded. The walled precinct of the old town is in shadow from mid-morning but adds a note of calm to the animated scene. Beneath the old town, there are older white-washed houses along the shore which give way to modest hotels and apartment blocks up to five storeys high at the other end of the double crescent of sand. Anything bigger than this is tucked further away from the sea, while all around the town is the clean outline of pine-clad hills. All day people clamber up the paths above the old town to the lighthouse which rises from the pines on the summit of the hill. The light changes as it has always changed at Tossa – deep green morning sea and deepest blue sky changing to pale blue sky and deepest azure sea as the sun dips well inland.

In the little cobbled streets of the old town, cats hold court amid the flowers, and from the lighthouse there are miles of typical Costa Brava scenery in either direction, wild rocky crags stretching south to Lloret and north towards Sant Feliu. There is a pleasant little museum and several art galleries and the scent of pine hangs in the air. Towards evening, the sun shines strongly down the valley behind the town, and illuminates the ancient walls in a pale, straw-coloured light of dry sherry. The near sea sparkles green and silver, the far sea is deepest purple. It is hard to object to all this, to feel anger at the passing of poverty and obscurantism. Tossa proudly flies the flags of Catalonia, Spain and Europe.

What one misses on the Costa Brava are those stretches of wild, unspoilt coastline that are such a feature of Cornwall and Devon, where mile upon mile of cliffs and coves have been preserved as part of the national heritage by the actions of the National Trust. It is difficult to feel like a traveller on this coast now, for everything is organised, all your needs are catered for, and to want something different from what is provided counts as wilfulness. The place that epitomised for me the limitations of the Costa Brava was Aiguablava. Even on a cold, grey April day it looked like nothing so much as a picture of itself: sea, rocky cliffs, bars and restaurants, pine trees everywhere. The much praised Cala Gelida turned out to be an urbanisation (Cala Gelida S.A.) of terraced houses and villas smothering the hillsides above attractive rocky coves. I did not stay long.

There is no doubt in my mind that the kind of private enterprise solutions that people find to mass tourism at places like Aiguablava and Cala Gelida are no answer to the shortcomings of places such as Blanes or Lloret, which cater for large-scale foreign tourism with large-scale facilities. Everything here is out of scale with nature – the massive apartment blocks and hotels, the nightclubs, the restaurants serving their own synthetic brand of local cuisine. But more than anything else, tourism has failed Catalonia because it has not, until very recently, been marketed as a separate cultural identity from Spain. The Spanish tourist industry has been a culture of exclusions, glossing over differences and producing a standardised product which can be enjoyed equally by British and Germans and Dutch, equally on the Costa Brava, in Mallorca or in the Canary Islands. Yet the Costa Brava is quite different from other parts of the Spanish coast, with a wealth of historical sites, for example, which other costas do not have. Inland, the green, fertile fields of the Empordà and the thickly wooded hills inland from Tossa and San Feliu contrast with the inhospitable, bare, sunbleached mountains that so often form the backdrop to the coastal resorts of Southern Spain.

Where the tourist is set to consume, the traveller probes beneath the surface of things. And just as I found confirmation at Tossa that all is not awful on the Costa Brava, so I found confirmation at Arenys de Mar that even on the Maresme, that crowded commuter coastline that stretches north from the fringes of Barcelona before petering out in the dry estuary of the Tordera at the extreme south end of the Costa Brava, all is not lost. If you must have a railway line and a main road along the coast, the last place you would put them is hard up against the beaches. But that is exactly what happens on the Maresme coast. A new motorway is promised which will take some, at least, of the traffic further inland, but at more or less any time of day, any day of the week, this coastal road is liable to traffic jams, or as the Catalans call them, 'collapses'.

Like many of the towns on this coast, Arenys is really two linked towns, one 'de Mar' on the coast, and another 'de Dalt' or 'de Munt' further up the hillside. In the case of Arenys, the two are joined by an exquisite sandy *rambla*, almost completely shaded from the sun and lined by a profusion of local shops, becoming increasingly touristy towards the 'Mar' end. The beach is tiny, and the showers a necessary precaution, but the fishing port is one of the largest on the coast, and there are modern sporting installations too. There are small boats which still use sulphur lights to attract their catch and modern trawlers fitted out with the latest in fishing technology. Sardines, lobster and red mullet are the basis of the catch, which is immediately auctioned at the fishing co-op on the quayside. There is a small, exquisitely furnished bar with nice lamps and bent-wood furniture. It is no surprise, on stopping here one night to take a rest from the main road traffic jam, to find that this doubles as a popular nightspot. Chairs and tables had been laid out where, earlier in the day, fish had been auctioned in a Catalan as richly incomprehensible as a fish auction in Japan, with market stall-holders in their pristine white smocks exchanging knowing glances with one another across the wooden boxes of ice and still-twitching fish.

At a bar on the beach, a group of Dutch tourists, men and women in their late twenties or early thirties, are celebrating their imminent departure. They have been coming here for ten years, much to the astonishment of the schoolgirl at the bar.

'Why are you so surprised?' I ask.

'Arenys is boring. Nothing ever happens here.'

'Oh I don't know, it has its attractions . . .'

'Perhaps.'

The bar is a family affair and the girl's mother pauses from polishing glasses to remark that young people want to be up and away as soon as they can.

137

'You have children. You know how it is. But she'll have to work hard at school and pass her exams first.'

The girl pouts, and turns to serve another customer.

There used to be hotels but they have closed, and fishing is now the main local industry. Like Vilanova, Arenys is attractive because it is real, a place to visit and get to know people rather than just a place to go for sea and sun and sex. The family at the café, the fishermen and the market women at the fish auction, the shopkeepers, the old people on the benches in the *rambla*, all have their tale to tell. And like many other small Catalan towns, it is a microcosm of Catalan society and the outside influences upon it: the Barcelona holiday-makers and commuters, the migrants from Andalusia and North Africa, the Dutch tourists. Yet it has a character which has been defined by its history of seafaring, in the Mediterranean, in the trade with America, in shipbuilding and fishing. And a great calm, which Arenys' favourite son, the poet Salvador Espriu, defined in a 1946 poem as:

> . . . l'ombra
> viatgera d'un núvol
> i el lent record dels dies
> que són passats per sempre.

(. . . the passing shadow of a cloud and the slow memory of the days which are gone forever).

Nearly at the other end of the coast stretching north to France is the town of Cadaqués, long the haunt of writers and artists, and definitely upmarket. And Cadaqués has managed to keep intact its very special profile, the church dominating a maze of little alleyways leading to and fro between whitewashed houses, all eventually falling to a number of linked coves overlooked by porticoed houses lashed by the stormy sea in the wet and windy Easter of 1969. Cadaqués in 1990 is not that different, despite the surprise of the sea lying calm and blue in the harbour rather than crashing in mountainous grey waves over the seafront. Additional villas and apartments on the approaches are complemented by an efficient traffic management scheme which severely restricts access to the older part of the town. In the old fishing quarter of Port Lligat, Dalí's house survives but encroaching building scales down its impact. Next door is the Port Lligat Hotel, square, solid and boringly predictable, where I watched the 1969 Boat Race on television while drying out from an adventurous excursion to the lighthouse at Cap de Creus. It was a bizarre experience: the ritual of England's two oldest universities rowing from Putney to Mortlake aroused no interest at all among the Catalans present, and in this setting seemed even more incongruous than the enormous white eggs that decorate the roof terraces of Dalí's house.

The harbour is busy with fishing boats, pleasure crafts and bathers, and the mountains that overshadow Cadaqués are outlined against a luminous curtain of haze. This coastline is intensely familiar because it is the scenery of some of Dalí's best-known paintings, including Glasgow's *Christ of Saint John of the Cross*. The rocks have been worn into eccentric and fantastic shapes by the wind and the waves, suggesting that Daliesque fantasy comes from without as well as from within. And changing social habits have added to the surreal possibilities of Cadaqués. As I sit pondering art and reality among the sea lavender and pinks, a large naked man, burned walnut brown by the sun, appears swimming strongly round the headland. He squats for a few minutes on the rocks to take his breath, like some modern Neptune, then plunges back into the turquoise sea and strikes out with strong rhythmic strokes across the bay towards the next promontory.

I have no particular preference for the eccentricities of Cadaqués rather than for the more predictable pleasures of Arenys. The traveller takes a country as it comes. And in Catalonia there is always Barcelona if you want life lived with maximum nervous energy and there are always the Pyrenees and their foothills if you desire solitude. What concerns me more, I think, is whether tourism, in its modern form, can ever be a really progressive experience. Because tourism invites you to view rather than to participate and experience, because tourism, at the end of the day, glories in sameness, not difference, and because tourism, in so far as it says anything about foreigners, speaks in cliché and stereotype rather than in realities.

This is not inevitable, which makes it sadder still. Paul Scott's novel *The Corrida at San Feliu* sums up some of the incongruities of tourism for me. Beautifully crafted around the metaphor of human life and taurine death, it begs a question: why a *corrida* at San Feliu, assuming that San Feliu is the Costa Brava resort of Sant Feliu de Guíxols? The rituals of blood, gore and death are of little interest to the Catalans. In Barcelona, Andalusian aficionados of the bullfight and foreign tourists still go to the bullring, but only the presence of foreign tourists has kept the *corrida* alive on the Costa Brava, as part of the packaged experience of Spain. Yet the author shows no hint of embarrassment about using such an obviously alien symbol in a Catalan setting.

And yet, and yet . . . It is too easy to blame the tourist, to make of the tourist another stereotype as blatantly inauthentic as the *corrida* at San Feliu or as blatantly obvious as the *sardana*. In the wonderfully bitter and moving and satirical eighth and final chapter of his novel *Señas de Identidad*, the writer Juan Goytisolo, born in Barcelona, living most of his life in France and writing in Castilian, compares the unreality of the tourists' view of Barcelona from Montjuïc in August 1963 with the reality of Spain under Franco and the fact that, within yards of where they are standing admiring the sights, the President of the Generalitat, Lluís Companys, was shot in 1940. It is a folk tale that has circulated in Catalonia by word of mouth ever since. But there was no stone in the castle to say that the President of the Generalitat had lived the last hours of his life there. Companys, the man who had come to symbolise Catalonia's opposition to Franco, had gone into exile in France in 1939, was seized by the Nazis when they overran France, handed over to the Spanish police, and delivered under armed escort to Montjuïc. He was summarily tried by the military authorities and condemned to death. The next morning he was put up against a bare patch of wall and shot. No-one knows what happened to the corpse, but probably, like that of so many other republicans, it ended up in a common grave in an old quarry in the Montjuïc cemetery. Goytisolo satirises pitilessly the bland story of Barcelona and its history told to the tourists by their guide, and their apathetic response. In the same August of 1963, I was making my second visit to Barcelona. I did not know about Companys. It takes time, as Goytisolo would, I think, recognise, to become familiar with what he describes as the 'chaotic geometry' of the city.

It would be ludicrous to suggest that all knowledge should suddenly magically land in the lap of the traveller. But there are, it seems to me, conditions that can be created. In the traveller

140

there is a willingness to experience, to find out about what is unique in a place and the sum of human experience which has gone to create the present. A special problem for Britain is our semiofficial status within the European Community as 'reluctant Europeans'. And it has deep roots. A 1986 European survey showed only forty-two per cent of Britons identifying the EC as 'a good thing' and twenty-seven per cent thinking it 'a bad thing'. The comparable figures for Spain were sixty-six per cent and four per cent!

Two things follow from this. Firstly, a desire to take our fill of sun, sand, sex and *sangría* with as small a dose of foreignness as possible. And, secondly, an extreme reluctance to make a serious effort to learn foreign languages, which I would argue is the *sine qua non* of travelling with understanding. In the case of Catalonia this means at least some Spanish and preferably a little Catalan, if only because the willingness to try a little Catalan does open doors . . . I was also very conscious of the difference between Catalonia in springtime and Catalonia in summer. In April people seemed to have both the willingness and the time to talk. In summer the pace can be frenetic indeed, especially on the tourist routes, and it is harder to strike up those casual relationships which help to define a country for the traveller.

Above all, contacts between nations must be contacts between people, real live individuals rather than abstractions of nationality, gender, race and age. My own first visit to Barcelona was as part of an educational exchange between English and Catalan students, a friendship which for me lasted well into my time of living there, until our paths separated into different interests and friends and priorities. The block of flats where they lived is still there in the shadow of Montjuïc, the only one in that street not to have been rebuilt, with the same old wooden lift with its polished bench beneath an enormous mirror. They were serious, hard-working people, the father a carpenter with a small furniture workshop, the mother a housewife, Jaume and his brother. There was a grandmother from Valencia who wore black as most older Catalan and Spanish women used to, but who had a glint in her eye and would occasionally tell stories about her girlhood on the Valencian coast which told of a less confined and rigid life style. Despite this, they introduced me to brandy and siestas, took me to the coast and the hills in the back of their hardy little Seat 600, and took me to watch FC Barcelona play Real Madrid, the great team of Puskas, Di Stefano and Gento. Years later, when we had stopped seeing one another, I would still occasionally see grandmother on her way to market near where I lived, and she would complain openly of the rigid way her grandchildren were being brought up, the rigours of their studies and the lack of fun in their lives.

My young Polish friend, who shared that unforgettable trip up the mountain to Sant Pere de Rodes, spoke neither Catalan nor Spanish, but was working within the context of a network of relationships deriving from English language schools in Cambridge. If Europe is to grow together as a set of linked nations with common histories and ideals, the ordinary people of Europe, and especially the young, must learn to live both with those things they have in common and those things which identify them as English, Scots, Poles or Catalans.

It is in this context that the role of those responsible for tourism in Spain becomes crucial. How can they help visitors to an understanding that goes beyond the clichéd and commonplace? Tourism during the Franco years was a centralised affair, and is especially connected with the name of the man who, from 1962 to 1969, was Minister of Information and Tourism, Manuel Fraga Iribarne. In his more recent democratic career as leader of the conservative Partido Popular (People's Party) and president of the autonomous government of Galicia, he prefers to be known as Manuel Fraga pure and simple. In a 1990 press interview in Mallorca he claimed to have no regrets about the development of tourism, a source of wealth in its own right but also a strategic factor which permitted other forms of economic development as well as widening mental horizons and getting 'our country' better known internationally. Leaving aside the environmental issues touched upon in this chapter and the next, it is this notion of 'our country' which I have suggested has been the most negative feature of Spanish tourism, especially for Catalonia.

While the Spanish National Tourist Office in London still puts out advertising material which lumps together the very different attractions of mountain and sea, coast and interior, Catalonia, Andalusia and Castile, local tourist offices in Spain are increasingly acquiring a strong local flavour. The tourist office in Girona, the best equipped in my opinion of all the local tourist offices in Catalonia, has a particular responsibility as representing the province which includes the Costa Brava, where many of the foreign tourists will have their first experience of Catalonia. It is to the coast that most tourists come. Yet the success of tourism in Catalonia, viewed as part of a project of re-establishing national identity, will be measured by its ability to attract visitors inland away from the international flavour of the beach resorts and to the more authentic centres of Catalan life. The progress of these efforts can be measured in some contrasting visits to old towns close to the coast.

Pals, between the pottery town of La Bisbal and the coast, is a good starting point for this excursion into the world of tourism. Its beach is the home of the gigantic red and white masts of Radio Freedom, which for years has been broadcasting the American version of The Truth to Eastern Europe. Despite Coca Cola, frequent visits by the American Sixth Fleet to Barcelona and US films on television, American influence in Catalonia is less pronounced than in the UK. The North American Institute in Barcelona has a considerable reputation for language teaching, exhibitions and cultural events, and Barcelona people speak well of New York as an exciting, vibrant city. Perhaps American culture is too different from Catalan culture to be perceived as a threat. The only thing to be said in favour of this stretch of coast is that the dense pine woods effectively screen the worst of the apartment blocks and camp sites and villas. Medieval Pals sits unhappily on its exposed hilltop, a tribute to the historical urge to recover and restore, but a comprehensive guide as to how not to do it. It all looks too new, too perfect, to be real. The modern paved streets are too hard on the feet, there are too many gift shops and too few bars. Real Pals is reduced to a roadside settlement of ugly blocks of flats. The only compensation for the steep, thirsty climb to the lookout point of El Pedró is the view of one of the most fertile areas of Catalonia, drained marshes which produce an abundance of rice and fruit and vegetables with distant views of castles and villages and churches and the Isles Medes off L'Estartit.

Yet only a few miles from Pals is Peratallada, an almost perfect example of what restoration can achieve. The first message is 'people are living here', a drift of wood smoke from a chimney, a face at the window, a supermarket and a post office in the arcaded Plaça de les Voltes. Everything here is stone, and most of the houses have massive doorways with stone lintels or, in the Carrer Major, arches. Peratallada is a place to relax in, with a pleasant open-air café in a gravelled square in front of the old castle and tasteful gift shops selling mainly glass and ceramics. The local policeman is very helpful in locating the church, an interesting Romanesque and Gothic structure across the road on the edge of the fields, with a splendid old straggling farmhouse next door to it. An old man engages me in conversation about his prickly pear:

'You see how the children attack it!'

'But it looks very healthy to me. I was just admiring it.'

'They slash it with knives, they try to carve their initials in it.'

'Your roses are lovely. And in flower already!'

Prickly pears seem to suffer in Catalonia much as beech trees do in England – I noticed even at the *parador* in Tortosa that people had carved their names in the fleshy leaves. His rambler roses, already in bloom on Good Friday, seemed to be more tourist resistant, and I was inclined to envy him his medieval house and roses rather than sympathise with him about his prickly pear.

This same balance of forces, of the everyday and the exceptional, the local and the outside world, I found later in the summer in the little Pyrenean village of Durro, with its Romanesque church, its gardens alive with apples, marrows and flowers, its farmers and its holiday homes. Sunday lunch time, the village bar, dominated by a stuffed boar's head, was as crowded as an English country local, with no single group dominant and a relaxed intermingling of local and not so local: farmers who lived and worked around the village, people born and brought up in the valley who were back for their summer holiday, and other people renting houses in Durro for the summer. It is a fragile balance, but one worth striving for. Elsewhere in Lleida province I found a genuine enthusiasm for the development of tourism. The enthusiasm may, of course, be closely connected to the lack of tourism Lleida has enjoyed in the past, but it was not only the obvious targets which were being pressed (the Pyrenean valleys with their Romanesque churches and winter sports facilities) but also less immediately obvious areas such as the dry lands south and east of the provincial capital. Under the heading of 'Route of the olive oil', the provincial tourist office, with support from the Generalitat, has produced a model leaflet outlining the special charm of these ancient towns and villages with their castles, churches and monasteries,

Jewish quarters and mills. However, there still remains a gap between the carefully produced local information of this kind and the large-scale advertising of Spain, including Catalonia, which appears in the press and on television in other countries.

A failure to bridge that gap will be disastrous in both cultural and economic terms. Catalonia is not as dependent on tourism as, say, the Balearic Islands, where tourism accounts for one quarter of all employment. Agriculture and fishing are both important, and there is the biggest collection of high-tech industry in Spain. Pujol has assiduously courted the Japanese and a number of Japanese firms are now well established in Catalonia. This is especially clear in the Vallès, immediately inland from Barcelona, with its university, science park and gleaming glass and steel factories. The saying used to be, 'Com el vallès, no n'hi ha res' ('There's nowhere like the the Vallès'). Now the farmland has become 'Silicon Vallès'. But a major crisis in the tourist sector alongside the continuing crisis of the textile industry could spell disaster for Catalonia. And these are exactly the conditions under which nationalism is most likely to be racist and inward-looking and least likely to be a dynamic factor in a new European settlement between the demands of the local and the international.

In 1989, for the first time since the depths of the European recession in 1983, there was a decline in the number of foreign visitors to Spain, and the all-important foreign exchange they bring with them. If 1989 was bad year, 1990 looked all set to be even worse. In the first fortnight of July, hotel bookings in Tarragona province appeared to be twenty-five per cent down on 1989. Given the exceptionally hot, dry summer in Britain and other parts of northern and western Europe, it is unlikely that the situation will have been saved by a late influx of visitors. On the other hand, there were some small indicators of improving future trends. For example, the Vall d'Aran was reporting an increase of fifty per cent in June tourists over 1989 and the prospect of nearly full hotels and camp sites for the summer. Girona province was also experiencing increased bookings for mountain camp sites and a general increase of interest in camping, despite the massive increase in camp site places from 50,000 to 130,000 in only four years.

There are, of course, issues at work here which have little to do with Catalonia. The new recession which crept up on Britain almost unnoticed in 1990 has obviously led to a decline in the most important source of tourists for Catalonia. Climatic changes, which may lead to improved summer weather in northern Europe and much less stable weather in the Mediterranean, are something that can only be reacted to not controlled. Concern about skin cancer has made it less likely that fair-skinned people from the north will want to spend a fortnight lying around on Catalan (or any other) beaches. And the Mediterranean has acquired the unenviable reputation of being the most polluted sea in the world.

Yet some, at least, of these problems are well within the competence of the Catalan authorities to solve. For example, the dramatic reduction in the number of British visitors to the Tarragona coast in July 1990 was not just due to economic recession in Britain, or the impatience of the Catalan police and press with the drunken hooligan elements of male British society who treat Catalan holiday resorts as their own private battle-grounds. People were reacting to the very unfavourable press given to sanitary conditions in the coastal resorts in recent years, sporadic outbreaks of avoidable illnesses such as salmonella and typhoid, and the 'accidents' at the local power stations, of which more in the next chapter on 'The Greening of Catalonia'. Furthermore, it was part of a general pattern of discontent in the province of Tarragona over subjects as varied as farm prices, industrial waste and nuclear power.

The depth and seriousness of these problems is such that it is impossible to imagine any 'quick fix' solution to them. Although I have described the Catalan government as 'conservative nationalist' it is not as ideologically committed on the economic front as the Thatcher governments of the 1980s here in Britain. This may be because the language question occupies such a key place in Generalitat thinking, but also partly because Pujol himself, through the crisis of his Banca Catalana empire, has had direct experience of the capacity of free markets to turn on their creators. But because the changes are major and long-term, they require a high level of co-ordination between different departments and levels of government. Clearly there will be a shift from mass organised travel to more independent travel; clearly there will be some shift from seashore to inland areas. However, other crucial areas include public health issues around the cleanliness of beaches and the disposal of sewage, the future of the Catalan nuclear industry, the future of the national parks, investment in training and tourist infrastructure.

Since a number of these items are dealt with in the next chapter, I will choose only one to write about here – the people who work in the tourist industry and are the human link between the industry and its customers, the human face of Catalonia for so many foreign visitors. The most noticeable fact, and one which is true of holiday resorts everywhere, is that the majority of staff are young, badly paid, temporary workers. It is not surprising, then, that stories of poor service and inflated prices abound. Yet the problem goes further than that in two ways. Firstly, that workers are only as good as their managers and that the level of training and expertise at more senior levels is not very high. And secondly, that a culture has developed in which tourists have acquired a low status. Their own inability to speak the local languages or understand local customs is a contributory factor, but there are deeper reasons, too, why foreign tourists are so often relegated to the back of the queue, kept waiting to do simple things like change money in banks or order a coffee in a bar.

As in other facets of Catalan life, I smell the legacy of Franco, of intolerance and chauvinism, and of an assumption that tourism was a means to an end rather than an end in itself, something that can enrich people's lives as well as contribute towards the economy. If tourism is merely a product, merely the connecting link between seller and buyer, then it is probably not worth bothering over. But it can be part of a process whereby the nations of the world learn tolerance and understanding.

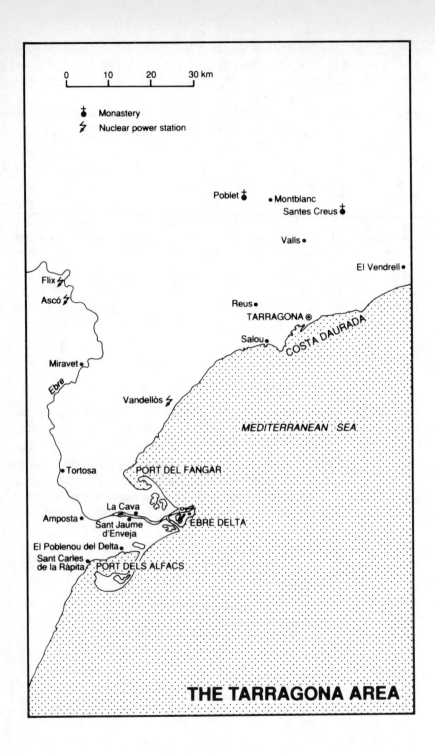

THE TARRAGONA AREA

Chapter 12

The Greening of Catalonia

Catalonia is a fertile, green, spacious and well-wooded land. But, as in all the advanced industrialised countries, the land is under attack, on the one hand from industry and the growth of big cities, and on the other hand from the increasing tendency to see agriculture as merely another industry. An additional factor in Catalonia is the pressure of tourism on the coast.

Catalonia contains only one of Spain's nine national parks. These are areas of outstanding natural beauty which contain important habitats for plants, animals and birds. Industrial, agricultural and building activities are strictly controlled within the confines of the parks, as are visitors. There are other ways, though, in which the greening of Catalonia works: efforts have been made to make Barcelona (and other cities) more pleasant and humane places in which to live; single issue campaigns centre mostly around pollution, especially of the sea and rivers; there is the nuclear power question; the disposal of industrial waste is a major problem. And finally there are questions of life style – is happiness the same as a high level of personal consumption?

But I want to begin this chapter in a very ordinary place, the valley of the Llémena just outside Girona. Coming down the valley, you can clearly see the façade of Girona cathedral standing high above the river. From in front of the cathedral you see nothing of the Llémena, except perhaps the slightest hint of a break in the continuous line of green wooded hills stretching away west of the city. The floor of the valley is intensively cultivated and there are a number of villages, such as Llorà, with its cluster of houses, its church with a slim, square tower and a large porch at the west end dated 1722. Next to the church is a carefully restored old house with a sundial that bears the inscription: 'Jo sense sol i tu sense fe, no som res' (I without the sun, and you without faith, we are nothing.)

The steep sides of the valley are thickly wooded with ash, elm and oak, the oak a mixture of both the deciduous northern species and the southern Mediterranean evergreen, which in spring creates a beautiful mottled patchwork of light new leaves and blackened old leaves. Above these woods are great limestone cliffs and crags rising to 450–600 metres. Once you are in the valley there is no easy exit, for the Llémena does not lead anywhere. The road eventually peters out beneath the dark bulk of the Finestres mountain. Two side roads allow precipitous exits sideways into the Brugent valley and then to Olot.

One of the main characteristics of the valley is water. As my friend Albert loves to say of the valley: 'You dig a hole and up comes the water.' Albert is a wiry, grey-haired man who combines considerable practical skills with spiritual concerns. After a busy day working on the roof, he would spend an hour in solitary meditation before settling down to a convivial evening around a roaring log stove. Teresa is a tiny, dark-haired Frenchwoman from Pau, a gifted linguist who speaks Catalan and English as well as her native French. They are gradually restoring one of the old *masies* of the valley, the old farmhouses shared by animals and people, masters and servants, which are such a feature of the Catalan countryside. In spring there is water in abundance, and the water which comes out of the hillside is as pure as pure can be. But in summer it dries to a trickle and they were busy putting the finishing touches to a small reservoir to provide them with water for washing and for watering the garden. They have given up their Barcelona flat and hope to live here permanently, although Teresa will continue for some time to be dependent on a teaching job outside the valley. Other people see the valley as a commuter home, travelling daily into Girona to work. Some *masies* and a few modern chalets are in use as holiday homes.

This particular *masia* is not atypical. It is solidly built from stone, at one corner taking advantage of the natural foundation of one of the many great boulders that litter the hillsides in these parts. There are few if any windows on the ground floor, which was dominated by a kitchen with high roof-beams and the family hearth and the stable for the animals. During rebuilding work on the roof a wasp's nest and a sloughed snake skin provided evidence of other wildlife with an informal share in the *masia*. Now Marcelino the cat, Nica the dog, a cock and a couple of hens

150

are the latest residents. In one corner of the building lived a family of farm labourers with a separate staircase to their bedroom above. One of the features of the *masia* is the enormous room at the top of the stairs, from which the bedrooms open. This looks at first glance like wasted space and yet in some ways was the most important symbolic part of the house – a space for weddings and funerals and christenings, the ceremonials of family life.

To some extent, the rural way of life goes on. Farmers plough and sow and harvest their crops – corn, hay and other fodder crops. But gradually this little world is changing and it is not altogether clear what sort of future this valley may have. The sheep have largely gone from the hillsides but the cows remain. Olives are no longer grown in the valley for other cash-crops produce a better profit. On Saturday nights the sound of cheerful campers echoes across the valley from a camp site by the river, mingling with the croaking of frogs. On Sunday mornings, cyclists and motorcyclists appear. There is evidence of shooting and fishing going on. Factories have reached Sant Gregori at the mouth of the valley, and from here there is a straight, fast road into Girona.

Yet on a still morning, when drifts of cloud hang in the woods while the suns warms to its task of dispersing the morning dew, the valley has a magic sense of peace and harmony. The cuckoo sings happily across the valley, its notes reverberating from one cliff to another. Magpies, tits, jays, woodpeckers and blackbirds are among the birds of the valley. In spring there are gentians, vetches, wild strawberries, buttercups and violets in the meadows, and by the roadside blue aquilegias, violets, cowslips and apple trees. In summer the valley is a mass of wild sweet peas and wild clematis that will be old man's beard in time for autumn, daisies and pinks, thistles and meadowsweet. The flowers, in turn, make the valley a paradise for butterflies. The down-side of this are the ants and wasps and mosquitoes, which also regard the valley as their home, and any stray human as potential victim.

The earth's crust is fragile. In early July there was a small earthquake not so many miles away at Ripoll. Albert felt a slight tremor as he lay in bed that night and thought nothing of it until he read the local paper. In a steep part of the valley, before it widens out into their part of the valley, is a shallow depression

151

almost completely circular and some 100 metres across which is reputed to be the sunken crater of an ancient volcano. Can the valley sustain all the new demands upon it? For example, in the Llémena you can still dig a well and up comes the pure cool water. In other parts of rural Catalonia, wells are having to be dug ever deeper and the water comes up bearing pollutants from modern chemical farming. At one level the countryside can be protected, and the Llémena would clearly benefit from the kind of protection that the Peak District has received, with controls on new buildings and industries (including tourism) and subsidies for farmers to adopt less intensive farming methods that give back to nature as well as take away from it.

But at another level the greening of Catalonia needs, too, a change of heart on the part of people themselves. Sports such as shooting and fishing and cross-country motorcycling are not compatible with a responsible attitude to the environment. Neither are family picnics and camping that leave their debris behind them. All of these are only too common in Catalonia. On the other hand there are hopeful signs. People like Teresa and Albert moving into the valley will care for it as well as enjoy it. Their neighbours have the oldest *masia* in the valley but power their house by solar panels on the roof. Another friend farms organically and is aiming at self-sufficiency on a small-holding in the shadow of Rocacorba, a 900-metre peak with radio transmitters on its summit which dominates the skyline north-west of Girona.

Juan is rapidly becoming one of the characters of the valley, riding to and fro on an ancient motorcycle loaded down with tools and equipment for the farm. It is not an easy life, with mosquitoes in summer, the *Tramuntana* in winter, and the nearest kindred spirits a half-hour bike ride away down a bumpy track and around twisting, climbing lanes. A second generation Andalusian from Hospitalet, a large industrial conglomeration near Barcelona, he speaks Castilian with a ferocious southern accent, but is equally at home in Catalan. Juan is an enthusiastic and anarchistic spirit who insisted on me inspecting his gleaming giant red tomatoes by starlight while the most savage mosquitoes I have ever encountered swarmed around me. *Integral*, a commercially viable Spanish monthly ecological review, has a large readership in Catalonia and creates a network of people with common values and interests, and it is this kind of individual initiative which is the necessary complement to any government action to protect the environment. At a consumer level, changing life styles are reflected in markets such as the Friday organic food market in the Plaça del Pi in Barcelona, which sells olives, cheese, jams and honey in the shadow of one of the best loved of the city's Gothic churches. Herbalist shops have not only survived but are increasing in number. Public slogans I observed in the streets of Barcelona included 'Posem verda la ciutat' ('Let's green the city'.)

The most obvious and serious threats to the Catalan environment are nuclear power stations. Two of these are in an isolated part of the Ebre valley at Ascó and Flix, eighty kilometres north of Tortosa and eighty kilometres south of Lleida. The other two at Vandellòs, less than thirty kilometres south of the holiday resort at Salou, are clearly visible to both road and rail travellers, and it is around these two that concern has centred. Vandellòs I has been closed since a fire in 1989, and has been refused permission to reopen since only some of the recommended modifications to it have been carried out. Five modifications were demanded, work on three started, but only two have been completed. The general opinion seems to be that it is unlikely ever to reopen. Worse still, since the Vandellòs stations are privately owned, it is difficult to see how they could ever be decommissioned, since there would be no income to offset the enormous cost involved.

Vandellòs II has a history of accidents since its opening, the most recent of which was on 8 July 1990. Although it was allowed to resume operating within a matter of days, the accident provoked a lot of negative publicity. It was pointed out that with the wind blowing from southwest to northeast, a radioactive cloud escaping from the plant would quickly have contaminated both Tarragona and Barcelona. The accident at Vandellòs II, happening as it did in the middle of a substantial crisis in the tourist industry on this coast, focused attention on the nuclear issue in Catalonia. It also coincided with the presence of the Greenpeace boat, *Sirius*, in dry dock at Barcelona for repairs before resuming its summer patrols of the western Mediterranean, recording and highlighting levels of pollution on the Catalan coast. Although many beaches on the Costa Brava have the coveted European blue flag, those in the Barcelona area are heavily polluted.

In general, the Catalan public has a rather low opinion of

nuclear power and this is reflected in the press. Even before the accidents at Vandellòs and Chernobyl, stories in the press tended to emphasise the problems associated with nuclear power. Critics of the Generalitat are certainly easier to find in the province of Tarragona than elsewhere in Catalonia. One commentator who has written exclusively on green issues explained to me his view of the overall land policy of the Generalitat: Girona and the Costa Brava clean and tidy for the tourist, Barcelona as the industrial sector, Lleida as an agricultural province and Tarragona for such delightful activities as nuclear power stations, rubbish tips and petrochemical plants. He emphasised the high level of secrecy in Spain on nuclear issues such as safety and costing. When the first Vandellòs accident took place, firemen were sent out without any antiradiation equipment and have since refused to deal with the plant. At the time of the Chernobyl accident, Spain was one of the few countries not to issue radiation figures, but subsequent enquiries have indicated levels of radiation above those permitted, even though Spanish permitted levels are higher than those in other countries.

The various grievances in Tarragona came together in a large demonstration on 15 July 1990. Apart from the antinuclear committee, the other organisations were protesting about plans to dump industrial rubbish near Montblanc, the possible redirection of the waters of the Ebre towards Barcelona, hospital privatisation plans and the theme park proposed for Salou to revive its flagging tourism. The Tarragona neighbourhood associations were demanding an emergency evacuation plan in case of an accident at the oil terminal just south of the town. The one missing group, as the press observed, was the farmworkers union (the Unió de Pagesos), who throughout 1990 were in conflict with the central government in Madrid about the depressed state of the prices of dried fruits and nuts in the Common Market. Their preferred tactic is to block roads with tractors – the bigger the road the more effective the protest.

The remaining groups were all protesting about matters which come within the competence of the Generalitat. Their greatest success had been in preventing the royal visit to Montblanc in April 1990. On the appointed day, the eve of Sant Jordi, I was fortunate enough to be in Montblanc myself, if not in royal company. In the arcaded town square, the Catalan flags were flying, each adorned with a small piece of black cloth as a protest against the industrial waste site the Generalitat had planned for them. One of the hereditary Catalan titles that Prince Philip was due to assume was that of Montblanc, but the local people had already made it clear that such a visit was unacceptable if he came accompanied by Pujol, the President of the Generalitat. Since Pujol clung like a limpet to the Prince during his Catalan visit, and since the police felt unable to ensure a safe visit in the context of a small medieval town crowded between largely intact old walls, the only solution was to cancel. Many of the local inhabitants went off to Cervera to make their feelings known to Pujol in the presence of the Prince.

That night there was a concert of Gregorian chant music in the church of Sant Miquel. Indeed, a more unlikely place than Montblanc for the site of an industrial waste plant or for a hugely successful political campaign is hard to imagine. The other flags flying in the town were the mauve flags of Sant Jordi, proudly proclaiming Montblanc as the place where Saint George killed the dragon. The other local event was the Third Medieval Week of Montblanc, a series of lectures, exhibitions, games, medieval balls and concerts, all centred around the legendary identity of Montblanc as the authentic location for the story of Sant Jordi, the princess and the dragon. But Montblanc is a town of contradictions: a young lad in denim jeans and jacket carrying an enormous medieval banner through the Portal del Castlà gate; the Angels Inn on the corner of the Street of the Jews, the site of an important medieval Jewish community; the only place in Catalonia where I saw posters and slogans on the walls for the old anarchist trades union, the CNT. Montblanc looks prosperous enough, but its prosperity is very recent. The town stagnated within its walls from the fifteenth century until the 1960s and was the scene of intense class warfare before and during the Civil War. What the whole episode suggested to me was that if opposition as fierce as this could arise in a rural backwater like Montblanc, then conservative nationalism as a political force (if not a cultural one) was likely to be soon overtaken by a harder politics in which green issues would be of major significance.

The energy question has always posed a problem in Catalonia. There is very little coal, and so from an early stage in the development of electricity there has been a high level of dependence on hydroelectric power. But this is not without its critics.

155

In order to secure sufficient heads of water for the dams, rivers which should be fierce mountain torrents are reduced to mere trickles. High up in the Vall de Boí, within the limits of the National Park of Aigües Tortes, there is hydroelectric power. The author of a recent Everest guide to the park lambastes this particular concrete monstrosity, pointing out that the values of the unspoilt countryside do not belong to anyone but are 'a social value which each generation has the duty to pass on intact to the next generation'. And it is hard to miss the installations as they are right next to the top car park, which is the limit of vehicle transport into the park.

Coming back from the Vall de Boí, we took the lovely curving road over the Coll de Perves to the other Noguera valley, the Noguera Pallaresa. There is an extremely large lake which stretches almost the whole fifteen kilometres from La Pobla de Segur to Tremp. But here there has been a specific effort to take advantage of the requirements of hydroelectric power by developing the lake for water sports and to provide camp sites and picnic spots along the banks. South of Tremp, this road is as wild as any in Catalonia. The road first squeezes through a gorge south of Cellers, with tunnels and rock overhangs, and then climbs high above the river as it cuts through the Montsec mountains. The road wound interminably first one way then another into the full heat of the summer afternoon. We were glad that day to reach the square at Balaguer and a long, peaceful, late lunch in the shade of the arcades. Solar power seemed the answer to Catalonia's power problems on that particular day, and infinitely preferable to what has sometimes been described as the easy option of simply importing power from French nuclear power stations, which currently produce more than enough for the domestic market.

The National Park of Aigües Tortes and Lake Sant Maurici covers 10,000 hectares of Pyrenean mountain and lake between 1,600 and 3,000 metres high, so it would be surprising if it was not impressive. The reality is stunning.

Access to the park is not easy. There is indeed a 'road' into the park from the Vall de Boí side. What is not pointed out clearly is that there are four to five kilometres of appallingly rutted stony track to reach the road. But I suspect this track is unlikely to be improved, since it persuades many visitors to use the park's minibus, jeep and guide services, based at Boí, rather than risk their own vehicles. At the entrance to the park we are given a leaflet with a few simple rules, and are instructed to stop at the first car park since the top one is already full. The flowers are magnificent already – blue and yellow Pyrenean thistles, yellow antirrhinums, scabious, harebells, wild delphinium and heathers. There is a good footpath along the side of a tumbling mountain stream, the mountains behind us and to the side are clad with pine and spruce, the mountains ahead bare and silent, their steep slopes covered with scree. Rhododendrons and raspberries and juniper are increasingly part of the flora, with Rose of Sharon beneath the pine trees, while in the meadow areas the colours are blue, pink and yellow – harebells, the small carmine pink and a tiny, tufted, yellow flower.

The Refugi Estany Llong is a homely little stone mountain refuge serving tea, coffee, beer, wine and soft drinks, sandwiches and bacon and eggs to walkers who sit round long pine tables. At night there is sleeping accommodation above, up a ladder and through a hatch. Then, almost immediately, the path reaches a small summit and there below is the Estany Llong, its water of the most complex blue I have ever seen, including shades of emerald green, purple, brown, grey and orange. The rest of the world here is very simple – a china-blue sky, the grey rock and two shades of green, light for the grass and dark for the pines. The bells of cattle and horses can be heard on the flat meadow at the lakeside, the wild horses perform excitedly, the cattle standing or lying peacefully as in some seventeenth-century genre painting. We find a quiet spot for our picnic, but by the time we have finished, a further twelve people have joined us, further evidence of the tendency I have referred to before of Catalans enjoying their solitude together! Bells up the hillside turn out to be a large herd of light-brown Pyrenean cows browsing through the pine trees. A few fluffy clouds appear but blow away again as quickly. But the refuge is a good reminder that at this altitude the weather can change very quickly and that snow in winter and sudden summer storms can turn a pleasant hike into a dangerous adventure.

If the balance between wilderness and public access seems to be relatively satisfactory in the case of the Aigües Tortes National Park, I am less sure about other areas of outstanding natural beauty in Catalonia. Aigües Tortes, designated in 1955, is the only area of Catalonia which enjoys national park status. Since

1980 the Generalitat has designated a number of wetland and mountain areas as natural parks. Protective measures are enforced to safeguard the environment, but agricultural activities are allowed to continue and visitors are encouraged to take an active interest in the natural environment. I visited three of these areas: the delta of the Ebre; the marshes on the coast between Empúries and Roses (Aiguamolls de l'Empordà); the Cadí-Moixeró park, which covers the mountains south of the Cerdanya. In addition there are environmental controls in operation on the Medes islands off L'Estartit, with their colonies of seabirds and coral reefs which can be viewed from glass-bottomed boats.

In all of these cases there are actual or potential conflicts between the conservationist aims of the parks and the realities of economic pressures. Much of the Cadí-Moixeró park is as remote and isolated as the Aigües Tortes. But on the south-facing side there is a strange twin-peaked mountainous outcrop called Pedraforça which contains one of the few coal reserves, or lignite to be more precise, in Catalonia. The park was designated in 1983 but the year before this, the Pedraforça massif was given protected status to prevent opencast mining of lignite. Yet there is now a plan, supported by the Environment Department of the Generalitat, to set up a power station at Saldes which will burn the lignite extracted from the mountain! In opposition to this plan are traditional *excursionista* groups who have long favoured this area for rock climbing, and more recent environmental pressure groups.

In the case of the Medes islands, control was clearly necessary to prevent over-use and exploitation by the tourist industry on the Costa Brava, and the Aiguamolls Park is similarly placed in an area of intense tourist activity. The story here is similar to that of wetlands throughout Europe, with agricultural interests wanting to drain the land to exploit the rich fertile soil. The landscape that this produces around the village of Sant Pere Pescador, of small fields (*closes*) surrounded by drainage ditches has an appeal of its own, but it is easy to see how little use this is to the large colonies of wading birds who traditionally inhabit these marshes. During migration time in spring, 125 separate species have been observed on the marshes in just one day. The geography of the park is extremely complex. For example, the Empúriabrava holiday complex with its villas and marinas is actually within the confines of the park, which spreads from the outskirts of Roses to the mouth of the Fluvià river. From here, one narrow band stretches upstream past Sant Pere Pescador and another arm south along the sand dunes to Sant Martí d'Empúries.

There is clearly scope for conflict at a park like Aiguamolls between conservation and tourism. But such conflict is likely to achieve a high public profile, as has happened with the plan to develop a large tourist resort on the fringes of the Doñona National Park on the Atlantic coast of Spain. In Catalonia, major concern centres on the Ebre delta, where the list of unresolved questions grows every year. It supports a large and varied population of wildlife including ninety per cent of the wildfowl which winter in Catalonia, yet there is at least some doubt in my mind about whether the Ebre delta could ever be described as a 'natural environment'. The delta as we see it today represents several hundred years of intense human activity which have turned its wild salt marshes into a rich agricultural area, particularly for the cultivation of rice. Paddy fields occupy three-fifths of the cultivated land. The first recorded attempt to grow rice in the delta was by Cistercian monks in 1607, but the most significant developments followed the authorisation in 1851 of a project to canalise the Ebre right up to Zaragoza. The canal cut to supply water to the ship canal was also used for irrigation and led to the development of the irrigated fields on the south (right-hand) side of the river. The area north of the river was developed after the opening of a second canal on the left bank in 1912. Thus the area of the delta in which fresh water predominates over salt water was increased.

The population of the delta has also increased significantly, from about 5,000 in 1850 to 40,000 today. Malaria was endemic in the delta until well into this century, and only brought under control from 1917, which involved further intervention with the 'natural' environment. El Poblenou del Delta was founded in 1947 but is already on its second name, having been christened Villafranco del Delta (Franco Town). The present mouth of the river is the result of floods as recently as 1937: for centuries before that the river had two main outlets, one to the east, the other to the south, which explains the existence of the two curious lobules of land at Punta de La Banya and Punta del Fangar.

The attractions of the delta are immediately obvious. In summer the whole area is a mass of waving light green stems of the rice plants, while in spring the paddy fields stand wet and lonely awaiting planting time. The farmers live in small, square

159

whitewashed houses and work from small, square whitewashed huts on the banks of the fields, ditches and irrigation channels. On a cold April day I sat in my van at the end of a track in the lagoon protected by the Punta del Fangar. Gradually the wading birds (avocets and herons), ducks and terns, frightened by my arrival, returned to their feeding, their busy activity mirrored in the still waters of the lagoon, broken only by the wooden posts which mark the extensive mussel beds. Eventually I found my way round to the sea, and a small beach with a couple of dozen windsurfers, all carefully protected by wetsuits from the biting northwest wind known in these parts as the *vents de dalt*, the winds from the hills. Further along the beach were signs warning people to keep off during the nesting season. This was the nesting season, yet there were motorcycle tracks disappearing off into the protected area, and no sign of any enforcement of the park regulations.

Later in the afternoon, I took one of the simple raft ferries across the river, a wide brown stream between luxuriant fields and gardens, and further downstream thick woods on either side. It felt like equatorial Africa more than Catalonia. There is a lot of market gardening on the south bank around Sant Jaume d'Enveja – lettuces, potatoes and artichokes were much in evidence – and I suspect that some at least of this is part-time farming by workers employed in the processing factories which have begun to appear around the delta, or any of the other small service industries that support a community of 40,000. And a community it certainly is: a few years ago I drove through Sant Jaume (I think it was Sant Jaume but I was hopelessly lost at the time) in the middle of its *festa major*. There was dancing in the main street outside the café, and from an upstairs window someone was literally hosing down the dancers in the streets below, who went on dancing as if this was the most normal thing in the world. I am sorry to say we wound the windows up and drove slowly on through the crowd with fixed smiles. There are moments when even a Catalan festival is not one's idea of having a good time! But on that spring evening, people were few and far between as I drove along the road between the salt marshes and the sea and its mussel beds in the direction of Sant Carles and terra firma. The sun was setting fast over the bare grey Montsià mountains in complete contrast to the flat, watery world I was passing through.

Established by Charles III in 1780, Sant Carles de la Ràpita is a monument to rationalism. It is easy to see why the Catalans, despite their abhorrence of Bourbon centralism, were able to begin their economic revival in the eighteenth century. The national virtue of *seny* (common sense, wisdom, understanding) found a clear echo in the monarch's desire to bring Spain kicking and screaming into the modern world. Previously, in 1778, the king had authorised the port (Port dels Afacs, protected from the sea by the sand spit of Punta de la Banya) to take part in the trade with America, and he ordered the building of a ship canal to Amposta, the last town on the river before the delta. A small fishing and holiday village with a few striking neoclassical buildings is all that there is left to see of these grandiose plans from the Age of Enlightenment. I hope the natural park of the Ebre delta will not go the same way.

Until 1940, twenty million tons of mud and slime were deposited each year in the delta. Now less than three million tons reach the delta, the rest being caught upstream of the various dams on this immense river which flows to the Mediterranean from the southern flanks of the mountains of Cantabria in Northern Spain. The reduced flow of water in the river is producing an increase in salination levels in the delta, thus reversing a historical process which has been to the benefit of both farmers and wildlife. There is also, and inevitably in our dirty age, pollution in the river which threatens the delicate ecosystem of the delta. Two threats remain. Firstly the repeated suggestions that Barcelona might solve its chronic water supply problem by taking substantial supplies direct from the Ebre as it passes through Lleida province towards the sea. In 1990, water rationing was threatened for as early as 20 May and only unseasonably heavy summer rains kept off this threat. In the event, the turning-off of public fountains was the only visible sign of the water shortage. If that threat is predictable, the other is less so – the possibility of contamination from an accident at either the nuclear power plants upstream on the Ebre itself, or the Vandellòs II plant, which on a clear day is easily visible from the delta. It is not a pleasant prospect.

Chapter 13

Artists of Our Times

Figueres is enjoying itself. The *Tramuntana* is blowing, there is fresh snow clearly visible on the Pyrenees. But it is Easter Sunday, that most joyous day in the Christian world, and Figueres is enjoying itself. The locals are at the Easter funfair in the *rambla* with the usual assortment of roundabouts, lucky dips, and tombolas. Some of them, mostly grey-haired women and balding men, are dancing *sardanas* in the *plaça*. The band is the youth *cobla* from La Bisbal, in their smart uniforms and keen to make a good impression. But up the hill a crowd is gathering. The mecca is the Teatre-Museu Dalí. The loud, cosmopolitan queue contrasts with the general sense of sobriety in the town. But Dalí is big business in Figueres, and for the first time there is reason to get off the train or turn off the motorway as you drive south into Catalonia. It is my first visit to Figueres. My previous experience of Figueres was limited to its railway station on the main line from Barcelona to France, where you could always guarantee a cold beer from the trolleys that patrolled the platforms. Business extends beyond the museum to include a number of art bookshops in the neighbouring streets, where you can buy postcards at twice the price they are selling them for in the *rambla*. But no doubt Dalí, showman, entertainer and entrepreneur, would have approved.

Part of the reason for the queue are the extraordinary (for Catalonia) opening hours of 1130–1715 (1800 in winter). So there is time to be amused at the headless statue of 'King Salvador' outside the museum and to note the contrast with the austere Catalan Gothic of the parish church opposite. There are pro-Catalan slogans in English on the walls, with the red star and Catalan stripes banner of one of the pro-independence groups. A joker has written underneath 'En Català si us plau' ('In Catalan,

162

please', one of the key demands of the nationalists in the 1970s and early 1980s).

The story of how the theatre-museum came to be set up is bizarre, as one might expect, and spans the period 1961–74. The actors included Dalí himself, General Franco, various government ministers, including Fraga Iribarne and local municipal figures in Figueres. Dalí gave three reasons for wanting the old ruined theatre, bombed at the end of the Civil War in 1939, as a museum. Firstly, because he saw himself as a theatrical painter, secondly because the theatre is opposite the church where he was baptised and thirdly because his first exhibition of paintings was in the foyer of the theatre. It matters little, I suppose, that Dalí's Catholicism has always been of an exotic and idiosyncratic nature and that the third reason is not strictly true. Fraga supported the museum because he saw it as complementary to the development of the Costa Brava as a tourist area, a decision which in retrospect has proved very accurate, given the enormous number of visitors the museum attracts. After several face-to-face meetings with Franco, the Spanish dictator approved the museum plan: no doubt mutual flattery played its part, while Franco must have been glad to find at least one Catalan artist who supported his regime.

The actual funding of the conversion and reconstruction of the bombed theatre was through the Ministry of Housing, using the fact that money set aside for reconstruction of houses in Figueres bombed and destroyed during the Civil War had never been spent. This, in turn, aroused furious criticism in Catalonia. One Barcelona paper criticised the logic of 'why Dalí, a millionaire, is being given nine million [pesetas] to build himself a "home" for after he's dead'. It was also pointed out that the nine million was the going rate for a major Dalí painting at the time. But a success it is, the most visited museum in Catalonia. On that Easter Sunday, the museum felt dangerously crowded. In trying to get away from an art museum feel, the theatre-museum provides little in the way of background information or even titles of works. This is unfortunate, for Dalí's paintings work habitually on a number of different levels and often the title is the key that unlocks the meaning. On a number of occasions I struggled to the bookshop to check on the titles of paintings by finding postcards of them. Towards the end of my visit I did find a room which explores his career as a painter, and reflected that perhaps the layout is cleverer than it appears. First the Dalí experience, and then, afterwards, a little art history. But there are irritating features such as the picture of *Gala looking out to sea*, which becomes a portrait of good old Abe Lincoln at twenty metres. This only works if you put two coins in a slot machine viewer, but as this is less than twenty metres away, it doesn't give the desired effect.

The best spot in the museum is what used to be the stage, sitting under the giant cupola which has become a feature of the Figueres skyline. From here you look out through the proscenium arch, across the stalls to the circles and gallery. The stalls are open to the sky with the top of the octagonal church tower peeping down above the gallery. The stage itself is dominated by a huge blow-up of Gala, dated 1947, set against the rocky cliffs of Cadaqués and Port Lligat.

The intention to poke fun at the stuffy atmosphere of most museums is clear enough, but the jokes do not always come off. In fact, the theatre-museum Dalí is a big joke, but it is not clear who is on the receiving end. Is it modern civilisation itself, with its consumer fetishism, or is it us, the gullible public, who have paid to be entertained this way?

Sometimes the jokes do work. In the courtyard-stalls is a mighty column of tyres with a tiny black and yellow model fishing boat perched on top. Blue globules of sea hang from the boat and there is a half-closed umbrella above it. There is also an old Cadillac with wax figures inside it, and a slot-machine-operated fountain that comes on every few minutes to fill the car with water. After all, this is a *plaça* and what more likely thing to find in a *plaça* than a fountain?

There is nothing especially surreal about Catalan society, yet it has produced two major surrealist artists, Miró and Dalí. Perhaps it is the very common-sense approach of most Catalans to life which allows as compensation a strong sense of the ridiculous, of those moments when the everyday appearance of things is suddenly reflected back as nonsense. The mirror is shattered momentarily. Miró satirises mercilessly the materialism of the Catalans, while Dalí, on the contrary, plays on their sentimental attachment to national images as diverse as the Catholic Church and the coastline of the Costa Brava. One of the features Dalí, Miró and Picasso share is longevity. This has allowed them to develop far beyond the styles that brought them early fame – Dalí and Miró's surrealism, Picasso's cubism.

164

Picasso's presence in Barcelona is a very public affair, though not every visitor realises it. It is his murals which decorate the outside of the College of Architects opposite the cathedral. Passing these every day of my life for quite a long period in 1970, I came to accept them as simply part of the townscape. Revisiting them in 1990, I was struck by the excellent condition they are still in, with their emblematic scenes of Barcelona's public life – the processions of Palm Sunday, the popular festival of Sant Medir, the Christmas market which takes place in the square between the college and the cathedral. It is worth venturing inside the college, too, where there are two more Picasso murals, one portraying a port scene and the traditional image of the three chimneys outlined against Montjuïc, the other *sardana* dancers against a stylised background of hills and mountains. The materials are the same as those used outside, a rendered wall, with the designs picked out in small dark grey pebbles set into mortar. School children are often to be seen at work in this space making complicated designs out of building blocks, while others watch an audiovisual display on the city's history and pore over maps and old photos.

There are a number of ways of exploring the presence of Picasso in Catalan art. One of the most relaxing, if you have started at the College of Architects, is to go round the corner to the reconstructed Els Quatre Gats, the café where Picasso and his Bohemian chums hung out, and where Picasso's first one-man show in Barcelona was staged in February 1900. Els Quatre Gats was more than just a café. Modelled on the Chat Noir in Montmartre in Paris, it operated more like a cabaret, with exhibitions, music (Albéniz and Granados both performed there) and theatre. The model of Parisian Bohemianism is explicit in Rusiñol's picture *The Bohemian (Portrait of Erik Satie in his studio in Montmartre)*, 1891, which was exhibited in the 'Homage to Barcelona' show, subtitled 'The city and its art 1888–1936' at the Hayward Gallery in London in 1985–6.

The Paris-Barcelona axis is crucial during this period, with most of the Catalan *modernista* painters spending time in Paris and many of them, such as Sunyer and Utrillo, spending very long periods there. So much part of artistic life was the trip to Paris that a painter such as Joaquim Mir stands out precisely because he never visited Paris. Paris was important because it introduced Impressionism (and eventually post-Impressionist ideas) to Catalonia and replaced anecdote by atmosphere as the substance of painting. But whereas the Málaga-born Picasso became a leader in the Parisian avant-garde art world, the Catalan painters preferred to develop in their own directions. These directions can best be explored by a visit to the Modern Art Museum, within walking distance of Els Quatre Gats. Or, in the case of Rusiñol and Casas, two founder members of Els Quatre Gats, by visiting that lovely old house by the sea – the Cau Ferrat in Sitges – where their paintings and a superb collection of Catalan ironwork and ceramics are exhibited.

As with so much of European art nouveau, there is a major influence from the English pre-Raphaelites. This is immediately apparent in the Modern Art Museum in the dreamlike pictures of Joan Brull or Adrià Gual. There is a generalised sadness in the turn-of-the-century art, but only Nonell, in his pictures of hunched figures in dark tones, achieves any real depth of feeling, the sense of the closeness of death and tragedy.

The further exploration of this darker side of life is left to Picasso. A key experience for Picasso was the suicide in 1901 of his close friend, the painter and writer Carlos Casagemas, with whom he had shared studios in Barcelona and Paris. Death and suffering dominated the Blue Period (1901–4), the part of Picasso's career immediately following his close association with Barcelona. Poverty, disappointment in love, illness and premature death are the other face of the high-spirited Bohemianism which characterised turn-of-the-century Paris and was reflected in the Quatre Gats cabaret in Barcelona. This period in Picasso's life is crucial to understanding him above all as an artist of our century, rooted in the wealth and poverty, the joys and sorrows, of great cities like Paris and Barcelona.

Picasso has been lucky with his Barcelona museum. It is installed in two Gothic palaces next door to one another in Montcada street, where the aristocracy lived cheek-by-jowl with rich merchants and traders in the Middle Ages. It has never set out to give an overall view of Picasso's development. The fact that it is here at all is a mark of the formative influence in Picasso's work of the atmosphere of Barcelona, where he only actually lived from 1895 to 1901. The initial gift was of the collection of Picasso's friend and secretary, Jaume Sabartés, to which have been added substantial further gifts by the artist himself, and some paintings from the Modern Art Museum. This makes a visit there a very special event, for there is much detail on his early work, followed by a series of clues to his later development. It is a museum which makes you want to see more.

The early drawings from Picasso's student years emphasise what a brilliant draughtsman he was. The pictures of the Blue Period are also well represented, including a portrait of Sabartés. But this period is, of course, characterised most by the pictures of the underworld of misery and exploitation and shadows, together with images that bring together the psychological torment and the physical reality of urban poverty.

Yet there is also much in the museum to remind us that the mature Picasso, permanently exiled from Franco's Spain, turned in later years and in a critical way to specifically Spanish themes, such as the bullfight and the fascinating series of forty-four paintings done in 1957 on the theme of Velázquez's *Las Meninas*, which draw out all the latent grotesqueness and human frailty implicit in the court painter's 'official' view of the royal family. Neither can the bullfighting prints be said to glorify Spain's traditional sport, just as in the College of Architects murals in which a young girl leads a bull, the female principle of harmony triumphs over male striving and civilisation lives on.

The Fundació Miró in Barcelona is different in a number of ways from either of the other museums so far described. Firstly because it was designed by the architect Josep Lluís Sert and is an important work of modern art in its own right. Secondly because of its site, high on the Montjuïc mountain, so different from the urban settings of Picasso and Dalí. But most important because it is run as a living cultural and educational centre rather than a museum (Picasso) or a spectacle (Dalí). The primary intention was to provide ample space for temporary exhibitions of all kinds. My own first visit to the Foundation in the first flush of post-Franco freedom and the early days of the Foundation itself was to a great exhibition of the Catalan cultural heritage and this remains an indelible memory. On an upper floor there is a lecture room and a library, open to all visitors. In the courtyard is a pleasant open-air café. Concerts of modern music, often first performances, are part of the overall work of the Foundation. So the Miró Foundation is a place to spend the day, especially if your visit, like my own most recent visit, is an escape from the infernal heat of a summer's day in Barcelona, the sort of day when even a trip on the air-conditioned metro is a treat.

The nicest route to Miró is along the Carrer Nou de la Rambla which opens off the *rambla* just to the seaward side of the Liceu opera house. Along here there is opportunity to survey the changing mood of this part of the old town, which is part of Barcelona's ambitious urban renewal projects. Two men with clipboards (urban planners?) pause to chat to a group of middle-aged prostitutes who have brought chairs out into the street to chat and take the sun. Out on the Paral·lel a sentimental passer-by has donated a bunch of red carnations to the well-known statue of the flower girl (La Violetera). From here the funicular climbs the hillside with glimpses of brilliant blue morning glory between the tunnels, and then it is a short walk to the Foundation.

There is much to admire at the Foundation. I was especially pleased to find that Calder's *Fountain of Mercury* is now in place, carefully sited so that you look out upon it, and then through a further glass wall to the city spread out below. The light part of the mobile, in constant motion, contrasts with the ponderous flow of mercury across black metal platforms. The sculpture bears the name of Almaden, the Spanish mercury mine which has supported the installation of the fountain. It was originally built in 1937 for Sert's Spanish Republican pavilion at the Paris International Exhibition, which also featured Picasso's *Guernica*, now safely installed in the Prado in Madrid, and Miró's *El Segador* (*The Reaper*). Almaden was the scene of fierce fighting during the Civil War and so the sculpture pays homage to the victims of the war as well as to the long-standing friendship of Miró and Calder.

There is a video presentation which tries too hard to emphasise Miró's Catalan roots, and which manages to make statements such as 'The number three has always played a significant role in Miró's work.' Again, there is no doubt that these are echoes in Miró's work of the fantastic creatures in the tapestry of the Creation at Girona cathedral, but can they be said to be 'responsible for' Miró's bestiary? Indeed, Miró's own enormous *Tapestry of the Foundation* (I cannot believe the closeness of the title is unintentional), which occupies a key position as you come into Miró's world through the explanatory exhibits, represents the artist's own very personal symbols of woman, star, moon and birds.

There is often an element of play in Miró, which makes it especially appropriate (from an Anglo-Saxon point of view!) that he died on Christmas Day. On my most recent visit, a French child suggested that some conical figures with eyeballs on the roof were Father Christmas. But just as children's fantasies can weave horror as well as joy, the same is true of Miró's paintings. By allowing the free play of the subconscious to dictate the forms that emerge in his paintings, Miró was able to create a world that was at one level very private, but which at another level can return both to amuse and haunt the viewer. If the images of rural Catalan life stay with him and reappear in the late sculptures, so, too, does the anger which exploded in his work at the time of the Civil War and reappeared in his work with theatre groups such as Els Joglars in the 1970s. Even during the years of strict censorship, when I lived in Barcelona (1968–70), the theatre managed to be both lively and subversive. A memorable performance of Genet's *The Maids* roused the audience to fever pitch as they recognised the political implications of the play. The anger of a repressed people found its expression in the theatre rather than on the streets, but Catalan theatre groups such as La Fura dels Baus and El Tricicle continue the tradition of satirical guerilla warfare on 'respectable' society.

The long space between the Civil War and the transition to democracy, when Miró worked largely on personal themes (the star, bird and woman symbols), from 1956 in a studio in Mallorca designed by Sert, is punctuated by an occasional, highly visible public work. An example is the *Sun* and *Moon* ceramic murals, created with another friend, the potter Llorens, for the UNESCO building in Paris in 1958. Pau Casals, of course, was also involved with the United Nations at the time, and Miró thus fits into that category of the Catalan who expresses in his work and life the importance of the universal as well as the local in the life of an artist, a human being.

Following Miró's death in 1983, it was decided to enlarge the Foundation to incorporate a permanent exhibition of the artist's own work. Space was also required for the beginnings of a permanent collection of contemporary art in memory of the painter, which exploits Miró's own longevity to represent the modern movement from Leger and Max Ernst through Roland Penrose and Anthony Caro to Tàpies. There is also a small but exceptionally clear exhibition of Sert's work, which clarifies the different stages of his career: his International Style buildings in Barcelona from the 1930s (the Casa Bloc and the TB clinic), his US work (especially the new buildings at Harvard); his later

European work (Miró's studio at Palma de Mallorca, the Maeght Foundation at St Paul de Vence in Provence and the Miró Foundation). It particularly shows how quickly Sert's career took off in the USA. He was President of CIAM (International Congress of Modern Architecture) in 1947 and Dean of Architecture at Harvard in succession to Walter Gropius in 1953.

The Miró Foundation is a living and lively place. In one room, a group of teachers on a summer course were working on 'expression', adopting poses which attempted to interpret the movement in the paintings. That sculptural, symbolic aspect was especially important in Miró's later work, such as the *Pagès català* (*Catalan peasant*) of 1968, where the symbols of nature and human beings in contact with nature join in criticism of the inhumanities of modern life as played out in both private and public arenas. Another such figure is the one with the hayfork, who presides over the terrace and pond in front of the building, and so, thanks to the exceptional placing of the building on the hillside, over the city itself. But these works themselves have their roots deep in the Catalan countryside and the painter's early pictures, as is made clear in the explanatory part of the permanent exhibition, which describes Miró's early career as a detailer of rural life, gradually emphasising those symbolic elements which were to recur in his work fifty years later. This also makes clear how loose is the description of Miró as a surrealist: he had personal but not programmatic links with the surrealists and was always his own person.

The final stop in this tour of the Catalan modern greats is also the most recent – the Fundació Tàpies just a block away from the Passeig de Gràcia. Although so close to the centre of Barcelona, it is as yet little visited; it is still the case that Tàpies' paintings are seen as difficult and obscure. Unlike the other three painters mentioned in this chapter, his images have not yet passed into the popular imagination. Born in Barcelona in 1923, he is part of the 'damned generation' who lived most of their adult lives in the repressive atmosphere of Franco's Spain. His early work was influenced by surrealists such as Miró and Klee, but in the 1950s he moved towards informalism, using materials such as straw and sand, and turning to collage. In the 1970s his work acquired a political cutting edge which placed him at the head of those artists who were demanding radical political and social change.

The building itself is quite remarkable, Domènech i Montaner's design for the Editorial Montaner i Simón publishing house. The fact that the building is lower than its neighbours has enabled the erection of a roof sculpture of coiled aluminium tubing, suspended from eight jutting girders. The auditorium itself is a vast double-height space well suited to the large dimensions of so many of Tàpies' works. One of the most striking features is the small, raised, external patio dominated at one end by a large black-on-indigo painting. On a second side are 45° vertical mirrors reflecting the sky, and at the other end a 45° horizontal mirror, which reflects both you the spectator and the picture. Doubtless there are different interpretations possible, but mine was something like the question: 'How does what you the spectator feel about the world around you measure up to how I the artist paint (image-ine) the world?' It is at that kind of cerebral level that Tàpies begins to have his impact and draw you into his pictorial world.

Tàpies has written extensively on art and cultural issues since the 1950s. These writings have been collected and published in book form since 1970, but the origin of many of them are articles written for the Catalan press. This makes them even more difficult to come to grips with because they refer both to Tàpies' own evolution as painter and thinker and to the particular intellectual and political moment of the article. Tàpies' own views on criticism are that the viewer of a painting requires initially a kind of critical spontaneity in response to the medium used by the artist, but that in order to understand the artist's reasons for painting a particular subject in a particular way some apparatus of art criticism is required. This makes it even more surprising that the Foundation eschews the sort of didactic approach which the Miró Foundation is so good at, presenting the paintings with little or no commentary or explanation. For example, a brief visit to the library/study area makes it clear that Tàpies has taken a special interest in Eastern art and philosophy; indeed, one of the objectives of the foundation is to act as a platform from which to launch the study of non-Western art. Thus, whereas his view on the importance of originality in art and his criticism of the so-called culture, which merely distracts people from the essential problems of their own existence and the world about them, are understandable from within a Western intellectual framework, the view of reality itself as an art form, the rejection of the humanity–nature dualism and the notion of creating beauty in our everyday lives and actions, require a different set of mental tools.

Tàpies' palette has changed little over the years. White, cream, ochre, grey cover the entire range of many of the paintings. They are, of course, the colours of so many Catalan towns and villages. I was especially struck by a painting called *Grey Ochre on Brown* (1962), where the colours were exactly those I had experienced a few evenings before, coming back into Barcelona in the twilight on the road that descends from Tibidabo. Colour is thus an event in Tàpies' painting and occurs as odd moments of vivid colour in otherwise subdued colour schemes. Some paintings are cryptic in their meaning, with much use of mathematical symbols, numbers and letters. But in other pictures a much more immediate emotional response is elicited. In *Earth on Canvas* (1970), soil is attached to the canvas as if gradually obliterating it, like the moment when the soil begins to cover the coffin in a grave. It will be like that for all of us, the artist seems to be saying.

Tàpies has always been a political painter, though the politics are much clearer in the writing than in the pictures. Both he and Miró were present at the 1970 protest at Montserrat when Catalan artists and intellectuals locked themselves in the monastery in protest against the show trials of Basque nationalists in Burgos. The exile of Abbot Escarré in 1963 had only temporarily dimmed the light that Montserrat cast over the path of Catalan history. This 1970 protest led to the setting-up of the Catalan Assembly in 1971, which succeeded in uniting different ideological and political tendencies behind a simple programme in support of Catalan self-government.

In *Concert* (1985), Tàpies uses black and white paint applied to newsprint stuck onto the canvas, in such a way that only a few pages are easily readable. These include 'The Sky in September', the television and radio programmes, the stock exchange, and a page which reports a case being brought in Burgos against the mime group Els Joglars for blasphemy. In his writings, Tàpies makes it clear that he supports a broadly Marxist analysis of society, but without excluding a philosophical quest inspired by Eastern systems such as Zen or Taoism. In accord with this, he sees the artist's role as being a *veu* (a voice) rather than a *portaveu* (a spokesperson) for a particular political party. Tàpies has remained an abstract artist, but has also collaborated with poets, singers and visual artists to produce book covers, posters and record sleeves. He remains a formidable presence in the Barcelona art world, an avant-garde artist who has never lost faith in the avant-garde.

I have chosen in this chapter to emphasise four figures who already belong to the history of Catalan art. But the cultural dynamism of Catalonia depends not just on these figures but on the existence of a lively artistic life based on a network of commercial and public galleries. At the bottom of the *rambla*, the Santa Mònica art centre is being developed by the Generalitat, showing foreign art on the ground floor, Catalan art on the middle floor, which is in fact the main floor with ramp access, and photography on the top floor. The Barcelona Provincial Council is also involved with its grandiose plan to redevelop the Casa de la Caritat (Workhouse) site in the old town as an arts centre. This will create the 'Five Cs' – Centre of Contemporary Culture for the first three, and the remaining two provided by Casa de la Caritat.

In case young artists in Barcelona forget, there is a large reminder in the Passeig de Picasso. The monument is by Tàpies, the words by Picasso: 'No, painting is not made to decorate apartments but is a weapon of war, offensive and defensive, against the enemy.' The satire on materialism is in a direct line from Miró's angry surrealism. The sculpture is a glass box, a 3-D development of Tàpies' collage work, inside which a fountain plays, if water shortages permit. On the roadside is a pile of old furniture with a cross feature very prominent. On the park side, the pile of furniture takes the form of poles and banners, and the difficult to decipher, but hard and stern message quoted above. I sit under a palm tree in the park. It is four o'clock and my arm is bubbling gently with heat blisters.

Chapter 14

Catalonia: Barcelona – Towards 2000

Quite by chance I acquired a book in Barcelona in July 1990. I was fascinated partly by the title (*La Nació Pura* – *The Pure Nation*), partly by the fact that it had been published in Llívia, the Catalan enclave in France. It seemed a publishing curiosity. Fascination turned to dismay as I leafed through my purchase over a cup of coffee. The booklet consisted of a speech made at a meeting of the mayors of the Cerdanya (both sides of the frontier) in 1989. It is a powerful collection of slogans. Alongside 'one person, one vote' the author places 'one nation, one state'. There is much talk of a new European settlement, and in the centre spread of the booklet is reproduced a map which shows what Europe might look like by 2020, with the Soviet republics achieving their independence, Yugoslavia breaking up and the small peoples of Western Europe – Scots (but not Welsh!), Catalans and Basques achieving their independence.

At one level this is not so far removed from my own view that, within a more interdependent world, there is more scope for vigorous local democratic units of all sorts to develop – cities, regions, nations. The crucial difference is that I identify the notion of the nation-state as a problem, indeed as the major problem of Europe today. There is no state in Europe which does not have more or less discontent minorities, outstanding territorial claims on neighbours, or both. From Finland with its Swedes to Spain with its Basques, from Welsh and Scots in the west to Ukrainians and Macedonians in the east, the sorry tale unfolds itself. 'One nation, one culture, one language' is another slogan of *The Pure Nation*. Yet as we have seen, there are large numbers of people in Catalonia for whom Catalan is not the everyday language, who have a different cultural identity, or, as I tried to show in the chapter on Popular Culture, can share different cultural identities at the same time. Catalonia is a nation, but like

174

all nations it encompasses different languages, cultural and ethnic groups. Not to recognise this is a recipe for disaster, a recipe simply to go on fighting the same old, stale battles of centuries past.

The author of *La Nació Pura*, Josep Dalmau, is a man of immaculate progressive credentials, a priest, a staunch critic in writing and in political action of the Franco regime. Recently he has set up a sanctuary of Our Lady of Ecology in the village where he is priest. This man recognises, as we all must, that we live in interesting times. Yet this speech (I cannot comment on his other writings) represents a misreading of the times, a failure to think through the implications of national identity in the modern world. Above all, and this is perhaps the point to widen the argument away from this one booklet, writings of this sort offer no way out of the cul-de-sac of essentialism – the kind of mystical view that there is some peculiar essence which is shared by every Catalan, or every English person, or every Scot. Life in the modern world is more complex than this. To be English or to be Catalan involves certain material conditions of life, certain cultural experiences, a certain set of mental constructs (mostly deriving from education), all of which change with time.

It is commonplace to talk of the global village. As Dalmau insists, it is a global village in which we speak our local languages, watch our local TV stations and so on. Yet there are great forces in the world today which transcend national boundaries. One is the power of multinational companies, the other the threat to the global environment from pollution and global warming. From this point of view, the project of Catalan nationalism remains what Xavier Muñoz, to whom this book is dedicated, described it as in 1984 – an unresolved problem. He points out that despite its statute of autonomy and its new democracy, Catalonia is more 'Spanish' and more 'Anglo-Saxon' than it was fifty years ago, partly because of the inroads made into Catalan language and culture, but also because of the way its economy has been bought into by outside interests. He sees that there is nothing to be gained by replacing the all-powerful state by the all-powerful multinational or the naked power of money. He concludes that only a project based on a participatory democracy at all levels of society can shore up Catalan national identity. And this must include local communities weighing up the pros and cons of a new multinational factory or a nuclear power station on their doorstep.

The day-to-day issues which affect people's everyday lives are both duller and more important than questions of national identity – jobs, houses, war or peace, health, the environment. As Pasqual Maragall, Mayor of Barcelona, has suggested, it is questions like 'Who pays?', 'Who does what?', 'Who checks that they have done it?' which should determine the relationship between Catalonia and Spain. I would argue that the same goes for the relations between Catalonia and Europe, or Catalonia and the world. Pasqual Maragall insists on the importance of retaining different levels of government – local councils, the Generalitat and the Spanish state. It is a view of government that involves checks and balances as well as division of responsibilities. For him, the overall objective is the improvement of the quality of life for people.

People expect different things from different levels of government, and although I recognise that conflict does inevitably arise between these different organisations, it seems to me that the way to deal with this is not simply to abolish one or other of these (as happened in London in the case of the GLC). This case needs, of course, to be developed to include the European element, which will assume an increasing regulatory role both over the creation of wealth (industry and agriculture) and consumer issues (quality and safety of goods, standard of services, environmental issues). The cement of a sophisticated modern society has to operate at different levels, from the village square to the European Community, including the many groups people identify with that give them a feeling of belonging to society in a two-way process that benefits the individual as much as the group. Catalan democracy is as much about the rights of Catalan women, Catalan lesbians and gay men, Catalan newcomers, and so on, as it is about the rights of the Catalan nation.

The future of the Catalans is inextricably mixed up with that of Europe. It is emblematic that the flag of Europe flies next to the Catalan flag throughout Catalonia, outside town halls, at hotels and camp sites, at popular festivities. In the past it has been the nation-state that has determined how the economy is run, the conditions under which wealth is created. But it is local government that determines how some, at least, of that money is to be spent to benefit the whole community, through housing, education, street-cleaning and so on. Local authorities deal directly with multinationals to secure investment and jobs for their local residents. In some ways the Olympics is emblematic of this. It is a city, not a country, which hosts the Games and the kind of improvements Barcelona has made and is making with a view to 1992 and beyond, often in very sophisticated deals with multinational firms, speaks clearly of the power and influence of the local in the world today.

The old guard of our own Conservative Party have identified the shift of power within Europe very clearly. They are quite correct that power is passing to Brussels, the power to determine the overall economic structure within which wealth is created and distributed. But what is disappearing is not the power of the nation, but the power of the nation state. And I do not regret its passing. It is highly likely that as the power of the UK government in London declines, we shall see important centres of devolved power appearing in Cardiff and Edinburgh, able to deal directly with both the EC and the multinationals. And, of course, giving people that sense of belonging and identity which matters so much and prevents the world from becoming dull and grey and uniform. In Catalonia there will always be a special edge to this because of the size and importance of Barcelona, though as I have tried to describe in this book, there is interdependence as well as rivalry between city and nation.

It is a moment of pause in Catalonia. The size and scale of popular mobilisation 1976–7 were unprecedented even in this country where so much history has unfolded on the streets. No-one who was there can forget the sight of the Passeig de Gràcia filled from side to side and top to bottom with flags and banners and people. Even in photographs it provides an enduring image of the will for liberty of the Catalan nation. The slogans of liberty, amnesty and statute of autonomy united the nation in a way that it had never been united either before or since. An important point has to be made here. The success of that popular mobilisation depended at least in part on the wide-scale support from people who were not Catalans by birth. They showed a wish to be integrated within the Catalan nation. What they have never shown is a desire to be assimilated. The unity of that historical moment is hard to reproduce. One of the saddest facts about Catalonia is the reluctance of many immigrants to vote in Generalitat elections. They see it as 'the Catalans' own business'. Yet

177

from my perspective they are as much Catalans as anyone. A Catalan project that includes all the people who live and work there is an urgent political necessity. This will include language and popular culture as integrating elements in society, but also as elements of rich diversity.

The picture is complicated further by a more recent immigration which includes black Africans from North Africa and the countries bordering the Sahara, mostly fleeing hunger and poverty but some fleeing war and political persecution. Their position in a society with a high level of unemployment is highly problematic. It is calculated that 160,000 out of 300,000 foreigners living in Spain live in Catalonia. Doubtless there are others who have overstayed work or residence permits or never applied for them. And it is in declining industrial centres like Mataró that they are particularly evident. When African workers from Catalonia joined 6,000 others from other parts of Spain at a demonstration in Madrid in October 1990, they found themselves facing a counter-demonstration of 4,000 right-wing racist extremists.

Immigration in Spain has traditionally meant the internal movement of people, especially from the rural areas of the south and west to the industrial centres of Madrid, Catalonia and the Basque country. Immigration from outside Spain is a recent phenomenon, and has coincided with high levels of unemployment, so that many immigrants from North Africa are reduced to finding what work they can in the twilight world of the informal economy. It challenges the Spanish state to make difficult choices about the kind of rights accorded to these new citizens, and practical questions about how to deal with issues such as overstaying work permits, illegal immigration and refugees. These apparently 'technical' questions are heavily overlaid with emotive issues around racism and xenophobia. At a European level, there is mounting concern that the Trevi group of European ministers, who hold regular meetings to try to co-ordinate policies on immigration, asylum and so on, are in practice likely to produce policies that actively discriminate against the poorer, non-white countries, much as existing UK policies do. And at the Catalan level, the challenge is there to politicians of all parties to establish a national project which is non-discriminatory and anti-racist. As Paul Gordon, Information and Research Officer of our own Runnymede Trust has written in his useful pamphlet *Fortress Europe; the meaning of 1992*: 'Small nations or states are not inherently less racist or more open to people perceived as outsiders than their larger counterparts.' The European dimension is crucial, but we must all engage with the question of what kind of Europe we want to see grow in the post-1992 world.

Within that new Europe, there are different views of how developments should proceed which reflect the power bases of the politicians involved. At the moment, key decisions are made by the Council of Ministers, which reflects of course the power of the nation states. There is a clear move to extend the power of the parliament, in which Catalan deputies sit side by side with deputies from the other Catalan-speaking parts of France and Spain. Catalan involvement is most obvious at the level of regional projects. The Generalitat forms part of the 'Europe of the Regions' project which links historical areas with important economic interests such as Lombardy and Baden-Württemberg. The Barcelona town council supports a parallel project known as Eurocities, which includes Milan, Birmingham and Frankfurt. They argue that the great cities of Europe have traditionally been the motors of economic development and correspond to regions which are not necessarily political and economic units. Thus the economic hinterland of Barcelona extends north to Toulouse and Montpellier, south to Valencia and west to Zaragoza.

At the end of the day, both Eurocities and Europe of the Regions are likely to extend Catalan presence within the new Europe. But I would not like to end on an inward-looking note. Barcelona in 1992 will be the focus of the world community. Writing this on the day after war has broken out again in the Middle East, the idea of the countries of the world coming together in friendly rivalry and comradeship is an enticing one. Yet many of those countries will be the poor countries of the world. All that money spent to bring the peoples of the world together cannot disguise the enormous and increasing divisions between rich and poor, North and South. Recession and war can only exacerbate these differences. So it is important to realise that Catalans are actively involved around the world in projects that challenge the inevitability of those divisions.

On a day of suffocating heat and humidity in 1989, followed by the daily tropical storm playing over the green hills around Estelí in northern Nicaragua, I was privileged to meet young people from five European countries – Holland, Spain, Germany, France and the UK – the sister cities of Estelí, including Sheffield and Sant Feliu de Llobregat, an industrial town in the Barcelona Metropolitan Area. They had come together for a work project which involved providing mains drainage and drinking water for several thousand people. This in a town which twice in the previous ten years had been severely damaged by bombing, once in the final uprising against the Somoza regime, and once by the Contra rebels. The message was clear. Europe must work together, not only for Europe but for a world in which peace and justice finally replace the gods of war and the scourges of sickness, poverty and exploitation. And the Catalans, who have always loved liberty, have a leading role to play.